Carving Eyes

By Jeff Phares

D1569319

Fox
Chapel Publishing Co. Inc.
1970 Broad Street • East Petersburg, PA 17520 • www.foxchapelpublishing.com

Publisher	Alan Giagnocavo
Project Editor	Ayleen Stellhorn
Desktop Specialist	Alan Davis
Cover Design	Keren Holl
Photography	John Brookins

ISBN #1–56523–163–6

To order your copy of this book,
please send check or money order
for the cover price plus $3.00 shipping to:
Fox Books
1970 Broad Street
East Petersburg, PA 17520

Or visit us on the web at
www.foxchapelpublishing.com

Manufactured in Korea
10 9 8 7 6 5 4 3 2 1

Because carving wood and other materials inherently includes the risk of injury and damage, this book cannot guarantee that creating the projects in this book is safe for everyone. For this reason, this book is sold without warranties or guarantees of any kind, express or implied, and the publisher and author disclaim any liability for any injuries, losses or damages caused in any way by the content of this book or the reader's use of the tools needed to complete the projects presented here. The publisher and the author urge all carvers to thoroughly review each project and to understand the use of all tools involved before beginning any project.

Table of Contents

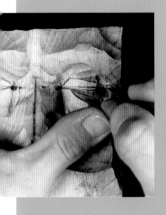 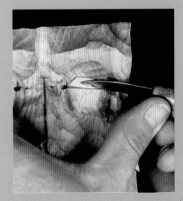 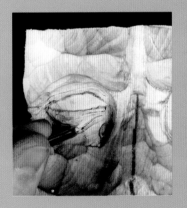 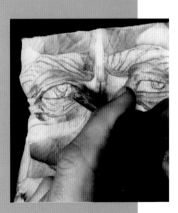

Introduction

Carving an entire human face involves a lot of study. Based on the feedback I have received from the students who attend my carving seminars, I believe there is a definite need among carvers for a series of books focusing on isolated areas of the human face. The book you are holding, *Carving Eyes*, is the second of three books that will provide an in-depth study of human features.

Why carve just an eye? That's a good question; one that is probably best answered by you. Perhaps you are an experienced carver who has noticed that the anatomy of the face you recently finished carving doesn't look "quite right." Or perhaps you are an experienced carver who has never tried to carve a human face before. Or you may even be new to carving all together and need a starting point for learning about carving faces. In any case, you need to look at carving just an eye as practice. Practice makes perfect—and it will help you to learn the process and make your future carvings more realistic.

Five Eyes

I have chosen to provide you with step-by-step instructions for five different eyes: a "regular" eye, a heavy lidded eye, a weathered eye, a winking eye, and a sleeping eye. By studying and comparing the steps involved in carving all five eyes, I believe you will learn and understand much more than simply following along with one carving demonstration.

As you work through each demonstration, you'll notice a lot of repetition. The "set-up" process is generally the same for any eye; once the underlying structure is set up, the processes start to change. I have deliberately chosen to repeat the set-up process for each eye because I believe that this repetition is important to help carving students learn the basics, and learn them well. If the underlying structure is not created correctly in the set-up process, all the detail in the world is not going to make the eye look right.

Before You Begin

First, along with the illustrations and photos in this book, you'll want to do your own study of reference material before you begin carving. Look for photos or models or other artwork of faces with prominent or unusual eyes. Get as close to your subject as you can. When I carve a weathered mountain man, I start with photos of mountain men. I familiarize myself with the different characteristics of their faces: noses, cheekbones, eyes, lips, eyebrows… Even though we are just studying eyes in this book, all of these other features come into play.

Next, you'll need to choose a piece of wood for your carving. I used a four-inch-wide basswood block in the demonstration. Why basswood? First, because the eyes are carved as a study stick. Basswood is easy to carve and will give you a good feel for the gouge strokes. And second, because it photographed well. In the demonstration photos, we lit the pieces carefully so that the shadows will highlight the gouge cuts.

As a side note, four inches is a little large for a typical eye. I am purposely carving on a larger block so that you can clearly see the different steps. The larger block also requires a larger-than-usual set of tools. I recommend that you practice on this larger study stick to perfect your skills before switching to the smaller scale of a human face.

And last, you'll need to assemble and sharpen the tools you'll need. Nothing will interrupt your creative flow more than having to search for and/or sharpen the right tool. Please note that I have been carving for years and have developed a liking for a number of specific tools. I use these tool repeatedly. You may have tools with which you are familiar. If those tools give you the same end result as the tools I use in the demonstrations, by all means, use them. It is not necessary to purchase a tool based on this book alone.

About Sharpening

As with any aspect of carving, I could go on and on; but for the purposes of this book, simple and effective are the two points to keep in mind when thinking about sharpening your tools. Regardless of the wood you're using or the subject you're carving, sharp tools are a necessity. As with anything, it is best to learn from the ground up. Learn to use a stone and a hand strop before you move on to other methods of sharpening your tools.

Getting Started

When you have chosen your wood and your tools are sharp, you are ready to begin carving. Apply the pattern to the block either by enlarging and tracing it or freehand. Take a second look at your reference material and review the gallery photos and anatomy illustrations in the book. Also, take time to review the diagrams in the back of this book as you progress. They will show you how to draw the areas you are working on and give you an overview of the process. Now, let's get started on carving eyes.

Overview

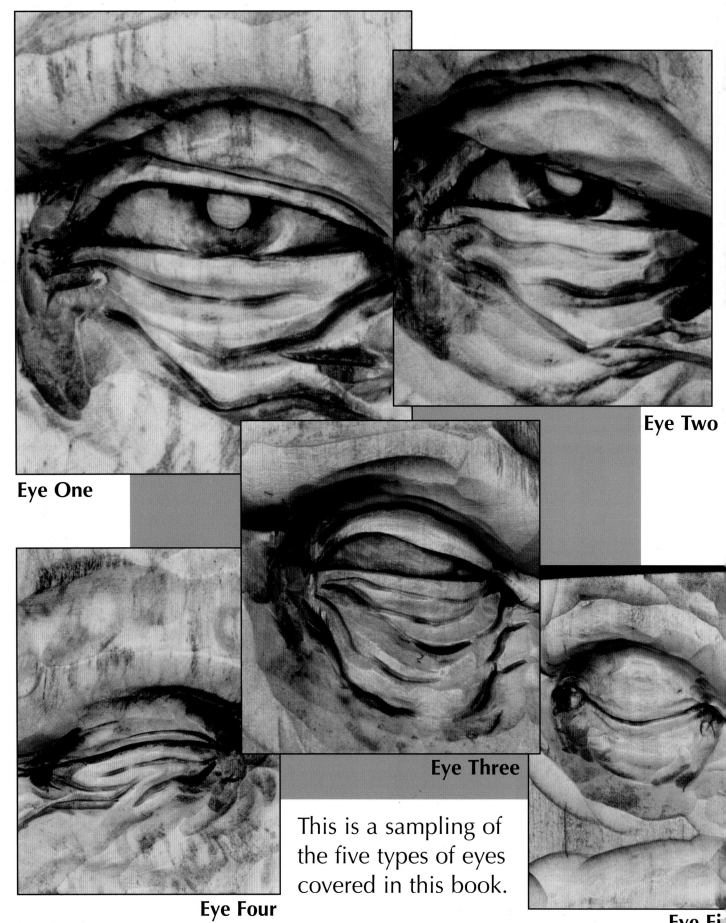

Eye One

Eye Two

Eye Three

Eye Four

Eye Fi

This is a sampling of the five types of eyes covered in this book.

Basic Preparations

The first steps of creating any eye are identical: You have to create the socket, the brow ridge, the beginnings of the nose, and the smooth transitions of form. Steps 1 through 23 show these basic preparations.

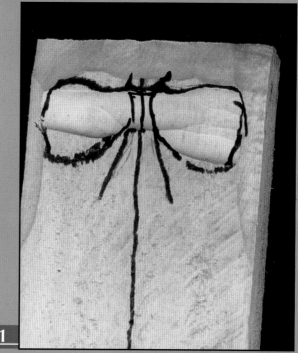

1 Draw on the brow ridge, following Diagram 1 in the back of this book as needed. Set your centerline; then sketch in the eye sockets, the brow ridge and the sides of the nose. Start to hollow out the sockets with a #9, 10 mm gouge.

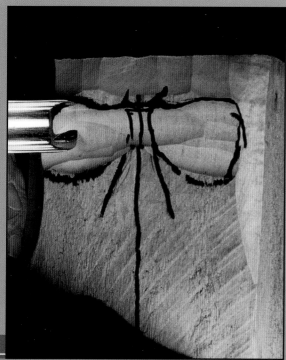

2 Use a #9, 10 mm gouge to create the sockets. The line at the top of the sockets marks the brow ridge, which is where the brow bones of the eyebrows are located. If you were working on a smaller face, you would choose a gouge that fits the size of the face. The smaller the face, the smaller the gouge.

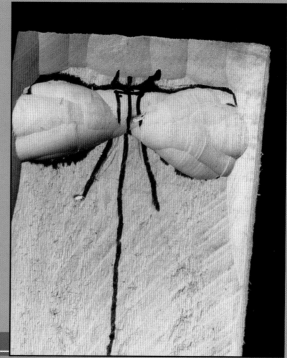

3 Here you can see what the eye looks like when the sockets are roughed in. Note that the eye sockets don't go all the way out to the edge of the block. Instead, they go all the way out to the knocked-off corners of the block. Follow through with your cuts.

Carving Eyes • 5

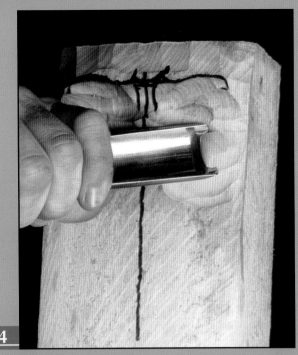

4

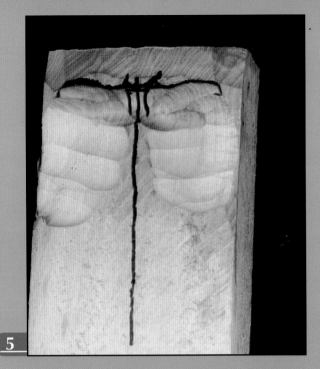

5

Use a #7 gouge to knock off the bottom edges underneath the eye sockets where the side of the nose and the cheek would be. Blend this area back to the socket. This creates a smooth transition from one area to another—key to creating realistic faces.

Take a look at the cuts that were made under the eye sockets. Notice how they create a transition between the two areas. (You'll note that I darkened the wood with water so that the newly cut area is more visible in the photograph.)

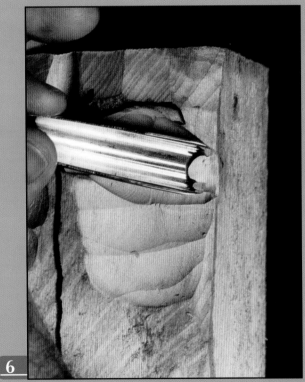

6

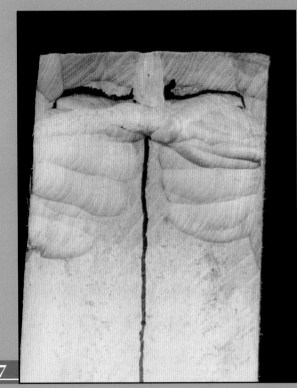

7

Using a #11, 10 mm, deepen the eye sockets again and make the separation between the brows. Remember, these eyes are quite big—almost lifesized—so that the wood removal process is clear in the photographs.

Here is the eye to this point. Notice on the right hand side of the photo how I deepened the eye socket. The left side has not yet been deepened.

8

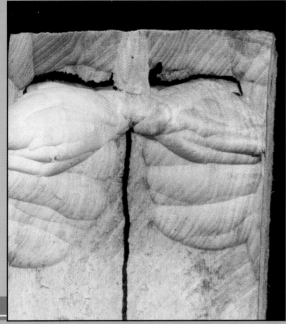

The eye socket on the left side has now been deepened. Notice how the cuts were made right off the outer edge of the wood? That forms the orbit of the eye as it comes around the corner of the face.

9

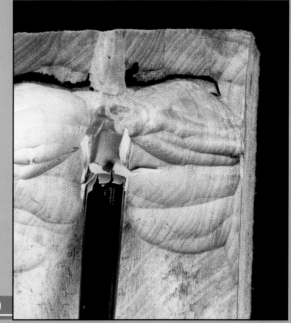

The next step is to set the bridge of the nose. Using a #7 gouge turned upside-down, round up the nose to create that dent in the brow ridge. The placement of the eye depends on the location of that dent. Notice how the corners of the upside-down tool are digging in.

10

Use a wide #7 gouge to create that smooth transition of form from the nose to where the cheek area would be. Notice that the marked-in brow lines are still visible. Always stay below those lines because that is where the brown bone is located.

11

Take a look at the eyes to this point. Notice the dent at the bridge of the nose and the smooth transition from the sides of the nose to the eye sockets.

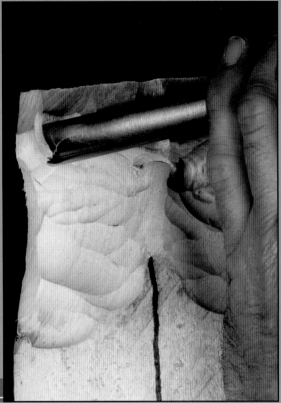

12 With a #7 gouge, work from the center to the outside to round the outer edge of the brow. This will soften the brow line a bit.

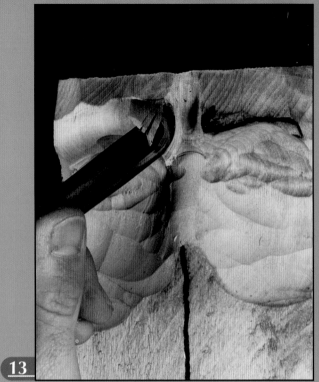

13 Now work from the center toward the nose. This will round the brow and create the crease in the brow. I am working here on the left side; the right side has not yet been carved.

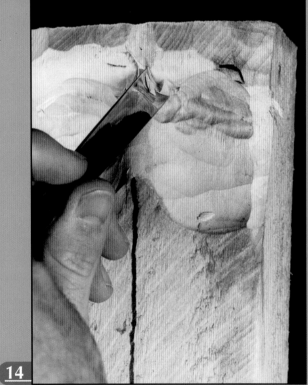

14 When you have completed the left side, move to the right side. Remember that the darkened wood is wet; fresh cuts show up as lighter wood and will help you see the area to be cut.

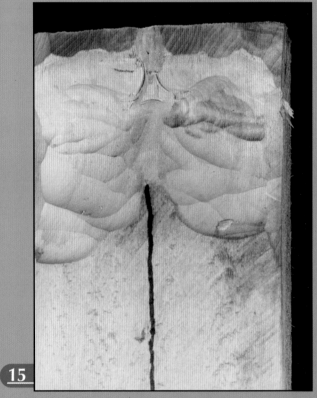

15 Here's a shot of the eye to this point. The three gouge cuts in the center clearly show the creases in the brow and the dent in the nose.

16 Using a #7 gouge, remove wood above the brow bone. Before you begin the next procedure, refer to Diagram 2 in the back of this book. It will show you the three basic cuts that are needed to refine the sockets.

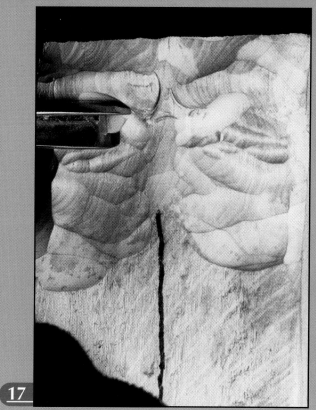

17 Still using the #11 gouge, remove a small amount of wood under the brow line as shown in the photograph.

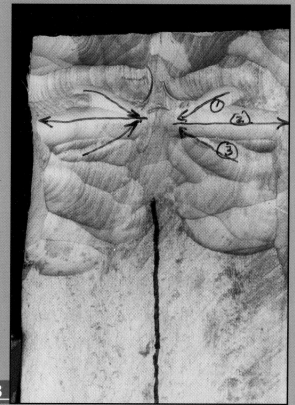

18 Make the second cut straight across the eye socket. In this photograph, I have drawn arrows in the directions of the cuts. Cuts 1 and 2 are made; you can see where the third cut will be made.

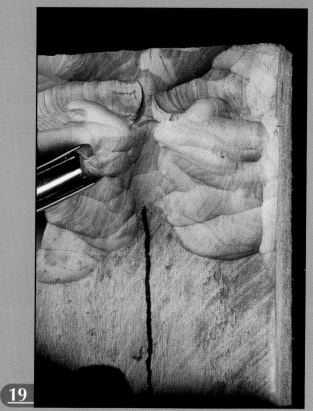

19 The right hand side shows the three cuts completed. On the left hand side, I am making the third cut.

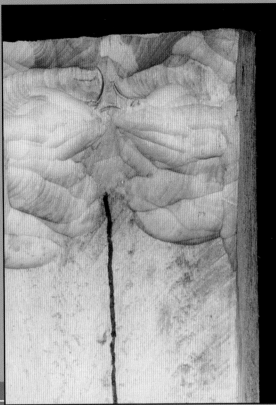

20

Here is the eye to this point. The sockets are deepened and the nose is still prominent.

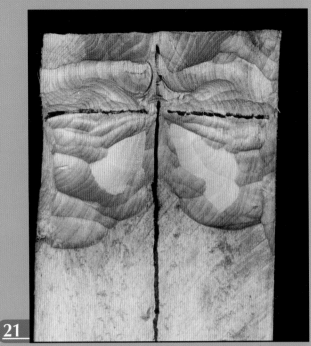

21

Draw in the vertical centerline down the middle of the nose. Refer to Diagram 3 in the back of the book for the placement of the horizontal centerline that runs across the center of the eyes. Remove a small amount of wood at the bottom of the eyes and the side of the nose.

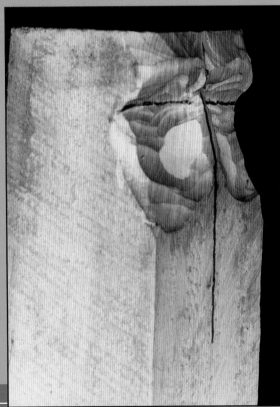

22

Check your carving from the side. A three-quarter view shows you the shape of the face, the depth of the sockets, the height of the nose and the brows, and the recessed corners of the block.

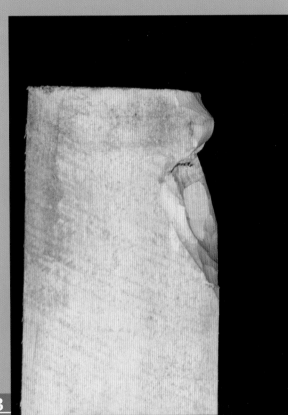

23

Here's a side view of the carving this far. Note how the orbit of the eye comes back into the face around the corner. The next step is to create the mound for the eye.

Creating the Mound

Up until this point, the steps for carving any eye are identical. But when you begin to create different types of eyes, the mound process, which is the next step, changes with each eye.

Remember, this first eye is a general eye with an eyelid and a few basic wrinkles. It's not a real young eye; it's not a real old eye. It is an average, normal eye that will work well on a variety of faces.

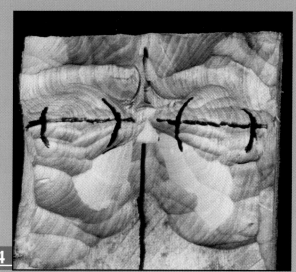

24

With a marker, make two semi-circle marks on the block to indicate the location of the mound. You will be cutting deep recesses between those marks, not circles. These cuts must be strong and correctly done to create a nice, round eye. Refer to Diagram 4 in the back of the book.

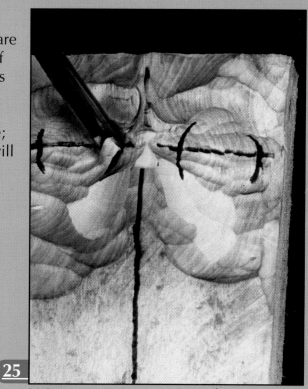

25

Using a #11, 5 mm gouge, dig in just under the brow line at the top of the cut. The depth of the cut should go into the face, not into the side of the nose. Cut right down to the centerline of the eye.

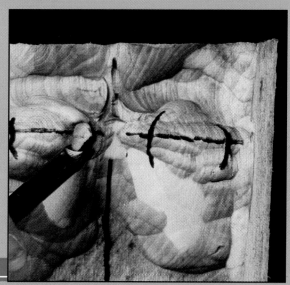

26

Cut up from the bottom to the centerline with the same #11 gouge. End your cut when you meet the end of the cut made in Step 25.

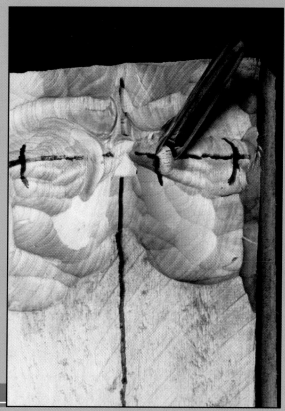

27

You can see the finished cuts on the left side. Proceed to make the first downward cut on the right side. Again, be sure to cut into the face, not into the nose.

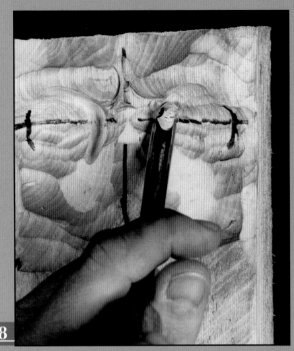

28

Make the second cut on the right side. This cut comes up from the bottom to meet the first cut at the centerline. It is important to keep both sides progressing at the same stage to keep the features even. Don't cut one eye mound to completion and then start the other one.

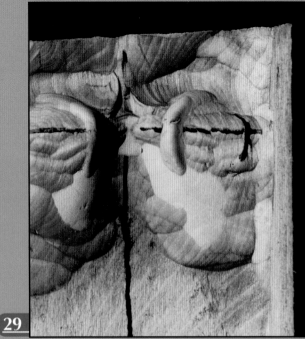

29

The two inside cuts are complete. Notice that these cuts are fairly deep. Go about as deep as your gouge can go. Don't be afraid to get some depth here. Without the depth, the mound will not be effective. Take a minute to go back and make the cuts deeper if need be.

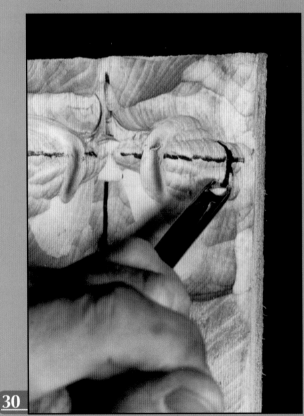

30

The outside cuts of the mound are cut similarly to the inside cuts. Start the cut at the bottom and end at the centerline.

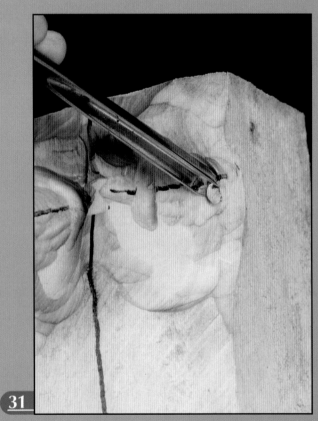

31

Cut down from the top to the centerline. The cut should be deepest at the centerline to create the deep corner of the eye.

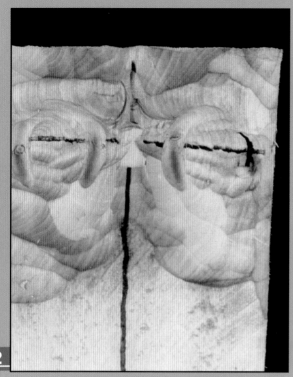

32

The outside cuts on the left side are
done; the right side has yet to be
completed. Complete the cut on the
right side and check the depth before
moving on.

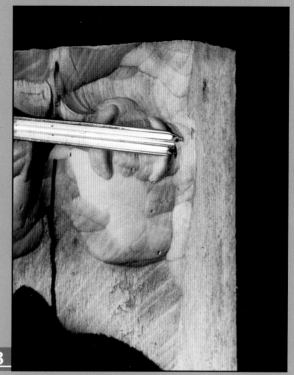

33

The final cut to set-up the mound is a
simple cut out to the edge of the face.
Cut from the outside corner of the eye to
the edge of the face. Use the centerline
as a guide

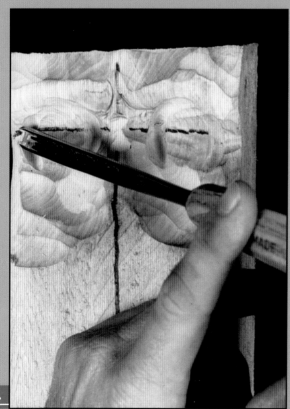

34

The cut on the right side is complete.
Make the same cut on the left side.

35

This photograph shows the finished set
up for the eye mounds. Notice how this
series of cuts has created the deep inside
and outside corners and the cut outs on
the outside corners of the eye.

36

Check out your carving from the side. If you have made the cuts correctly, you will be able to see the mound (the section inside the eye where the eyeball itself is going to be) and the orbit of the eye (marked with arrows).

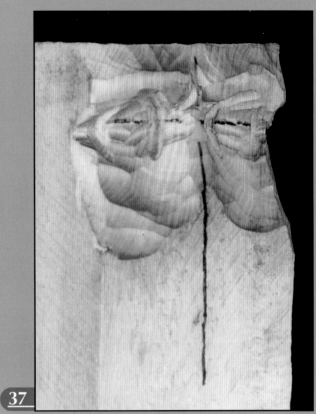

37

A three-quarter view shows the shape of the face where this eye area is. Notice how the eye area goes back into the edge of the face quite a bit.

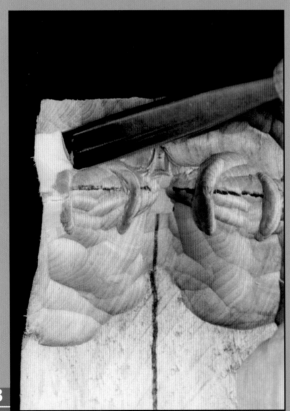

38

At this point, redo the brows and "soften up" the bottom edge of the brow bone where it meets the top, outer edge of the eye. Use a #7 gouge. Start at the center and work toward the outside.

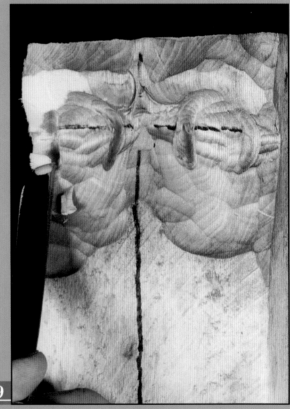

39

Using the same #7 gouge, round off the bottom side of the eye orbit to shape the bone there.

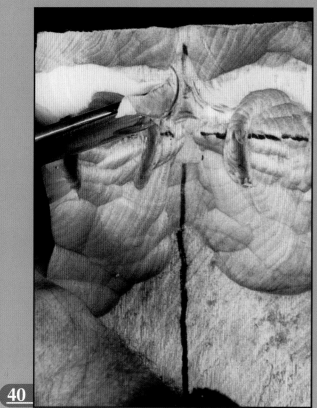

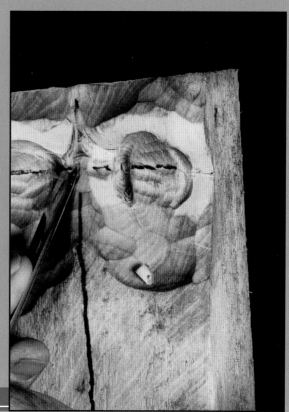

40 Starting at the center again, work in toward the nose. Essentially, you are recreating the same cuts for the brow creases that you made in Step 13.

41 Remove the chip at the nose by cutting up to the end of the previous cut. I am working on the left side; the right side is done.

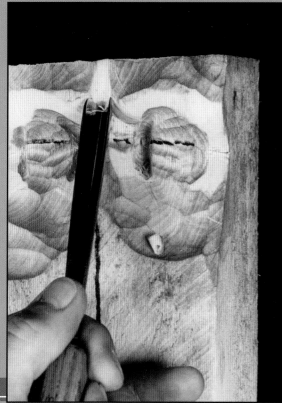

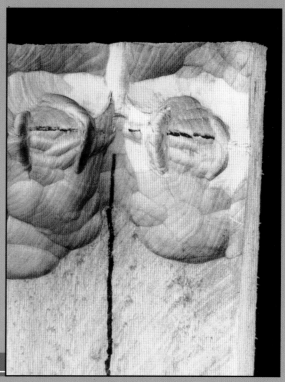

42 Take a #11 or a #9 gouge and split the brow. This is simply a little "ditch" that follows the centerline from the brow up to the edge of the block.

43 This photograph shows the eyes to this point. The light-colored wood shows all the wood that was shaved off in the past few steps. Notice how the centerlines of the eyes are still present. No wood has been cut away from the surface of the eye.

44

A side view shows the eye mass from the side. Notice the smooth transition from the brow bone to the eye socket. In the next steps, I will show you how to round the eyeball.

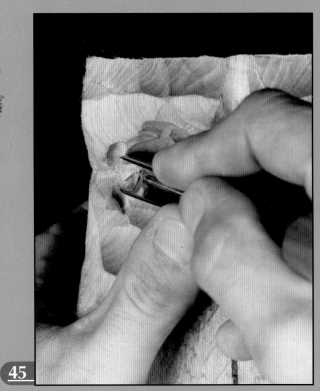

45

Using a #11 or a #9 gouge, remove small bits of wood at a time. Work from not quite the center of the eye down into the corners. Every cut needs to be as clean as possible from here on out.

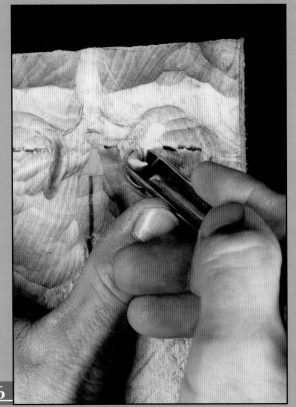

46

The left side is completed. Move to the right side and round the inside edge of the mound.

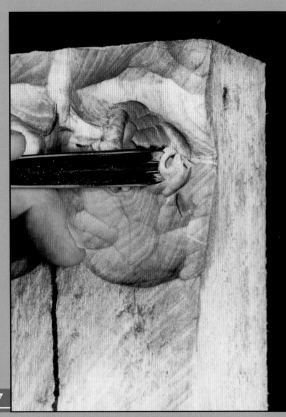

47

Continue to round the inside and outside corners of the eye, removing small bits of wood at a time.

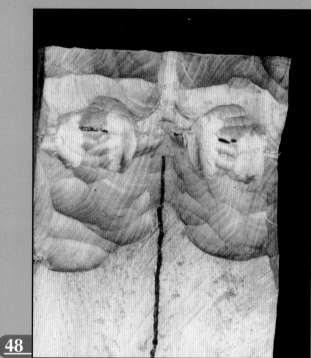

48

The light-colored areas in this photograph show where wood was removed to round the eye mound. Notice that the centerline is still intact in the center of the eye; no wood has been removed from the center of the mound.

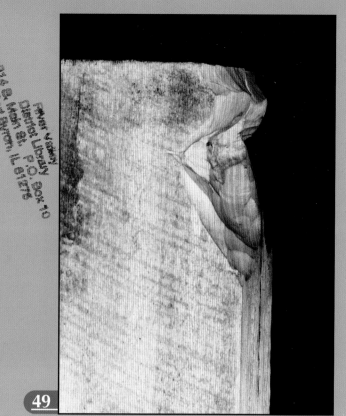

49

A side view of the piece shows the rounded areas. Notice that the surface of the eyeball itself is straight up and down.

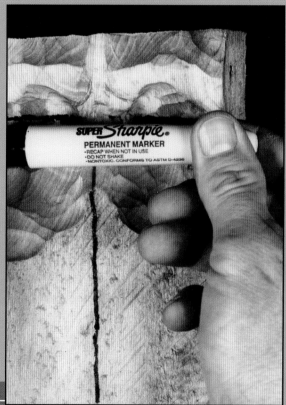

50

Use a marker to check that the center lines are even straight across. Next, check Diagram 6 for rules for the width of the eye and for the eye shape.

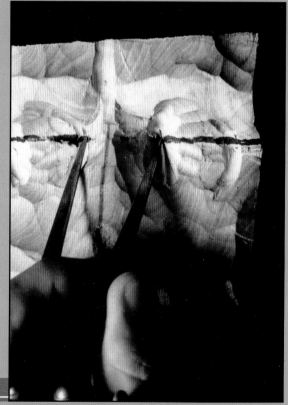

51

Use calipers to measure the width of the eyes. Here I am measuring across the center from inside corner to inside corner.

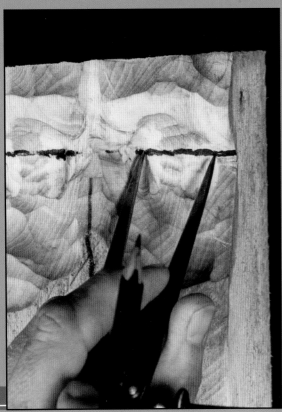

52 Mark the right eye.

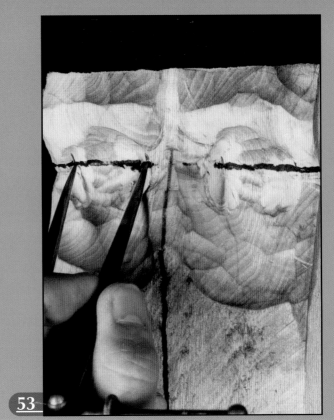

53 Mark the left eye. The calipers come in handy here to make sure that the measurements for both eyes are exactly the same.

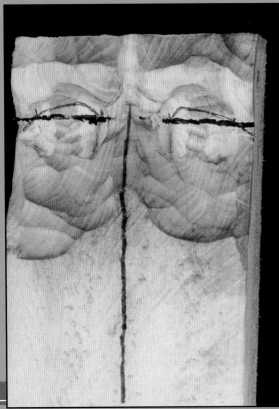

54 Draw the top eyelid on freehand. Notice how the top eyelid starts out away from the nose; it doesn't butt right up against the nose.

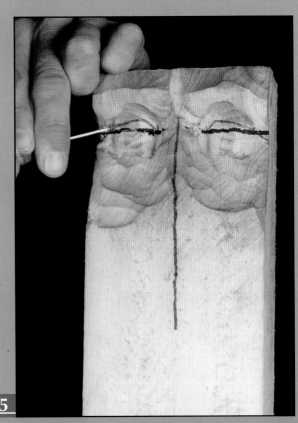

55 Using a knife, make a stop cut along the line for the eyelids. Start at the center and cut toward the outside corner.

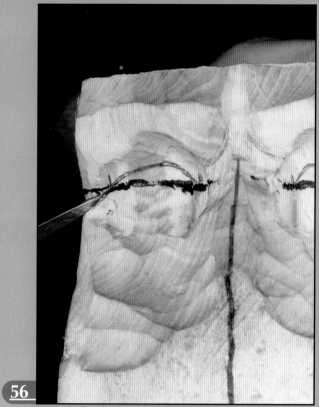

56 Carry the cut right through the centerline of the eye, out over the cheek and through that deep cut we created earlier at the edge of the eye.

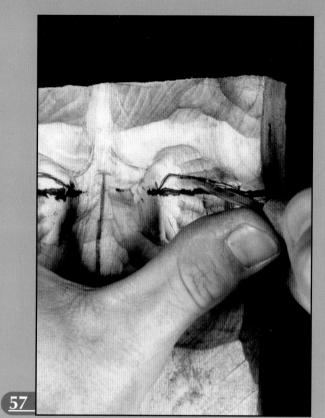

57 Make the same stop cut on the opposite eye.

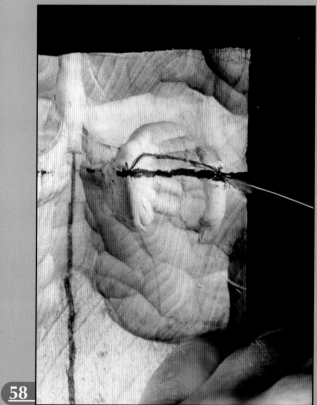

58 Again, carry the stop cut all the way through the deep cut at the edge of the eye.

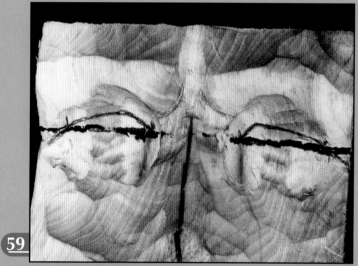

59 A close-up shows the stop cuts on the top eyelids. Notice how the centerlines extend past the corners of the eyes. These act as reference points. By not including them, you risk carving an eye that is too wide open.

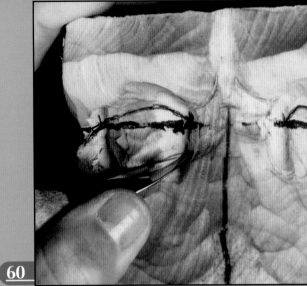

60

With a carving knife, cut in and straight up as explained in Diagram 7 at the back of this book. The key is to start low, way down where the bag of the eye will be, and cut all the way up into the stop cut at the eyelid. You already have a round eyeball, so be sure to maintain that roundness. Do not flatten the eyeball or take more wood off the center than you do on the sides.

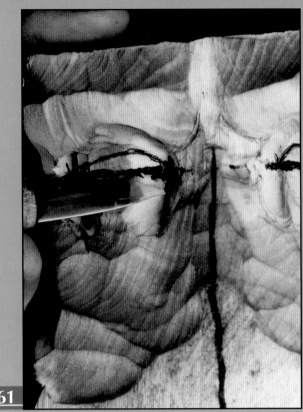

61

Continue the cut. You can see how I started at the bottom and am now halfway up to the stop cut

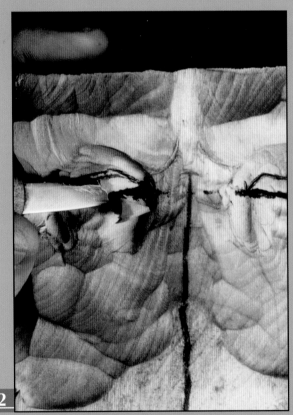

62

The chip will start to come out as the edge of the knife reaches the stop cut.

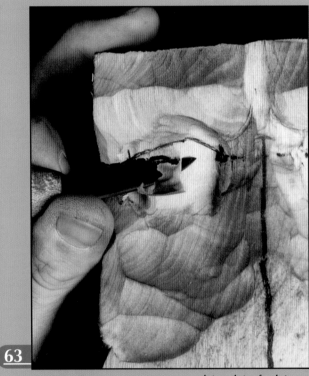

63

Continue to remove wood in this fashion all the way across the eyeball. Here you can see how I have removed wood from the inside portion of the eye. Your goal is to set that whole bottom area of the eye and the surface of the eyeball to help establish the eyelids.

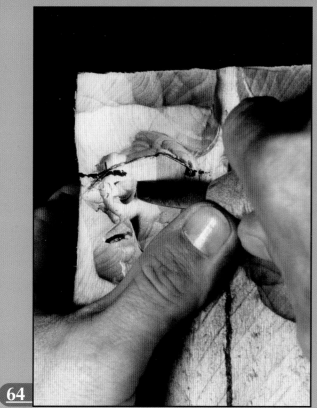

64 Continue the cuts right around the eyeball.

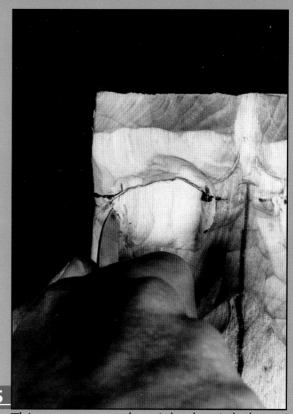

65 This next cut can be tricky, but it helps to keep the eyeball round and deepens the outside corner of the eye just a little bit. Start the cut at the outer edge of the eyeball.

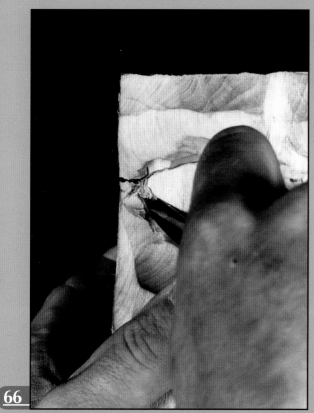

66 This is midway through the cut.

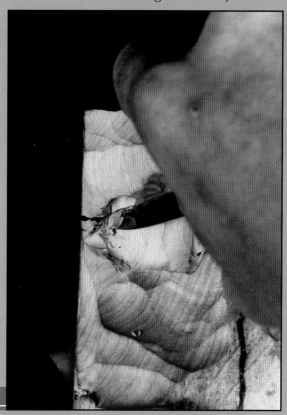

67 The cut ends at the top eyelid. This is one continuous cut. You have to swing and twist your knife around to create this.

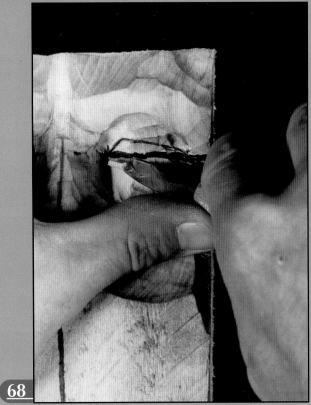

68

Remove wood from the surface of the eyeball on the right side. Notice how low I'm starting before I come up to the top eyelid.

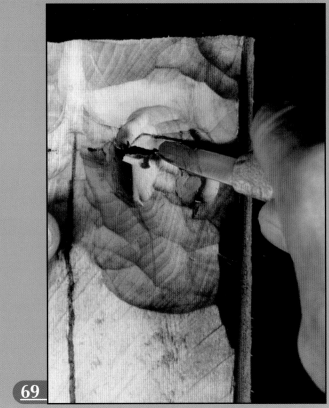

69

Finish the cut at the stop cut.

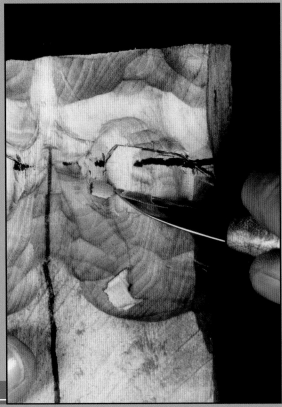

70

Continue removing the same amount of wood all the way across the eye. Be sure to maintain the roundness from side to side that you had already created.

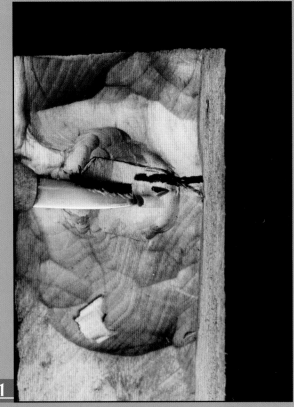

71

The last few cuts are made on the outer edge of the eyeball.

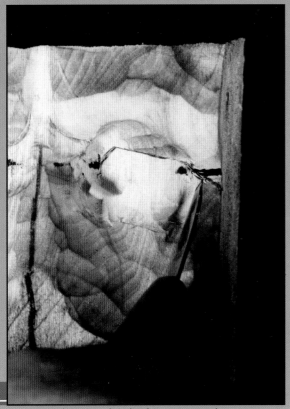

72 Repeat that tricky little cut on the outer edge of this eye. The cut starts here.

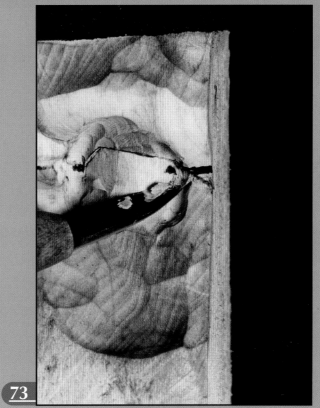

73 Midway through the cut your knife should be here.

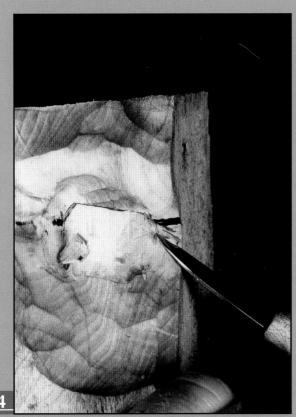

74 End the cut at the stop cut along the eyelid.

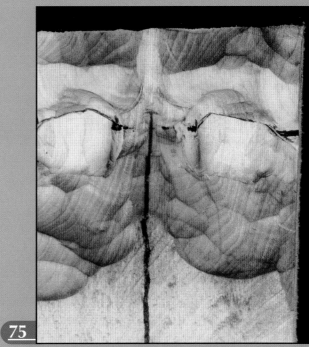

75 This photograph shows the eyes to this point. Notice the eyelid: It's just a millimeter or two thick. Also notice the eyeball: It's not pushed back very far. A common mistake people make is to angle the eyeball in toward the top eyelid. Make sure you cut in low and go straight up to it as explained in Diagram 7.

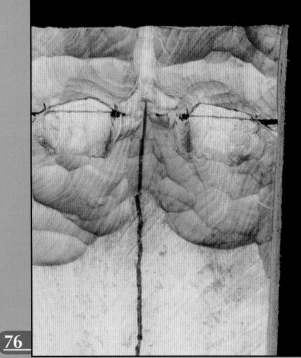

76

Redraw the centerline of the eyeball. Notice how the original centerline acts as a reference point. Can you see how you might be tempted to lower the centerline if you were to redraw the centerline without the benefit of the reference point?

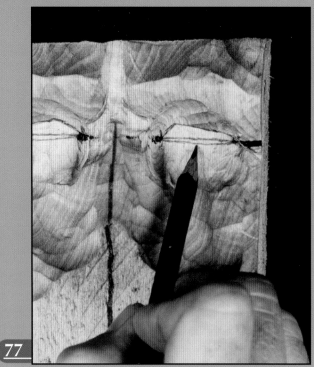

77

Draw on the bottom eyelid. Notice how close the bottom eyelid is to the centerline. The reason is that all the movement on an eyeball takes place with the top eyelid; the bottom eyelid stays in place unless the eye is winking.

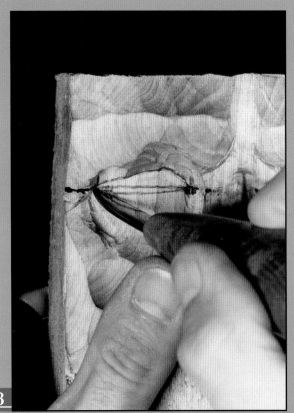

78

Using a carving knife, make a stop cut along the line for the bottom eyelid. Cut from the outside corner to the inside corner.

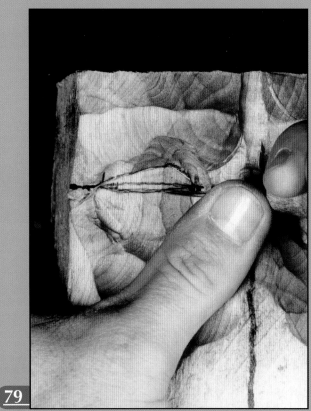

79

Continue the cut along the line, outside corner to inside corner.

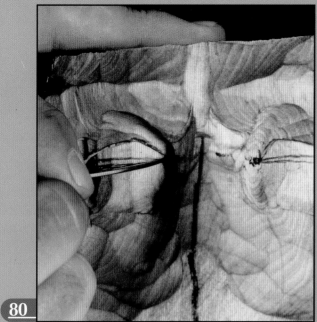

80

When you have finished the cut, make sure the inside corner is nice and neat by making a small cut from the inside corner into the already-made stop cut. Make sure your knife is very sharp before you do this step, and make sure it's a one-time, very small cut. The more cuts you make, the messier the eye will be.

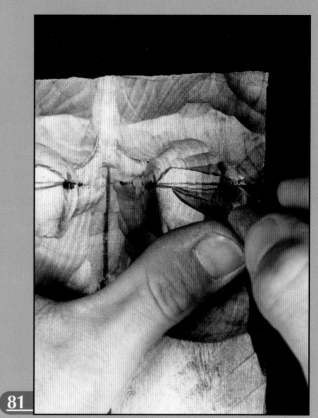

81

Make the stop cut on the bottom eyelid of the right eye.

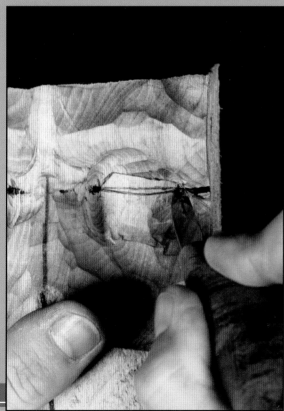

82

End the stop cut here in the outside corner of the eye. Notice how the bottom eyelid tucks under the top eyelid on the outside corner.

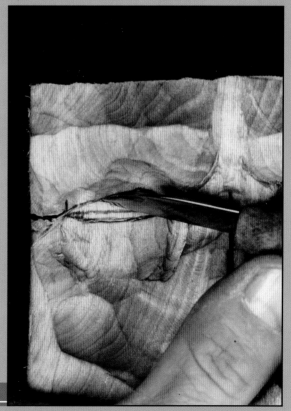

83

The next step is to relieve the eyeball. This is done with only downward cuts from the top eyelid down to the bottom eyelid. Cut in at the top eyelid.

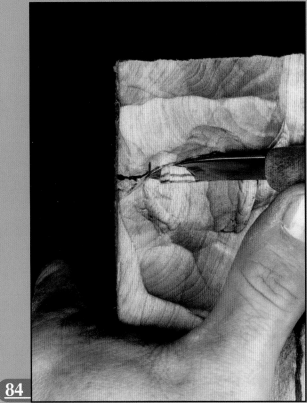

84

Cut down toward the stop cut at the bottom eyelid. This chip is just about ready to come out.

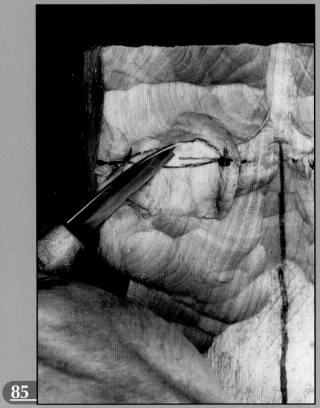

85

Again, start at the top eyelid and shave down only. I cannot stress this enough. Never cut up to that eyelid again.

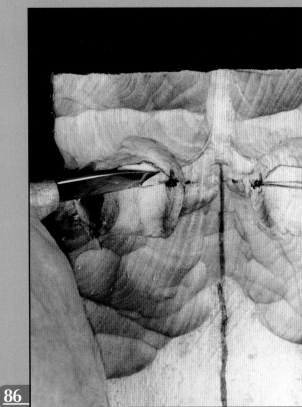

86

Remove the inside corner with the tip of your knife.

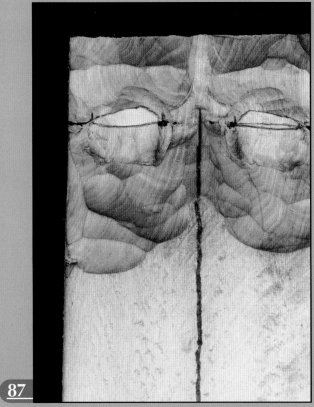

87

The left eye is complete; the right eye has yet to be finished.

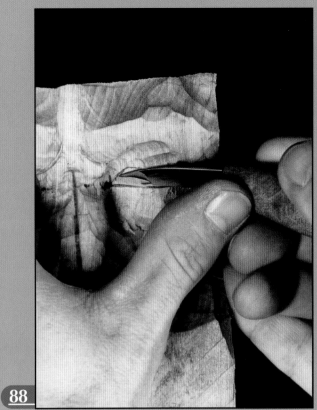

88

Make the same downward cuts on the right eye. Remember to always cut down from the top eyelid to the stop cut on the bottom eyelid.

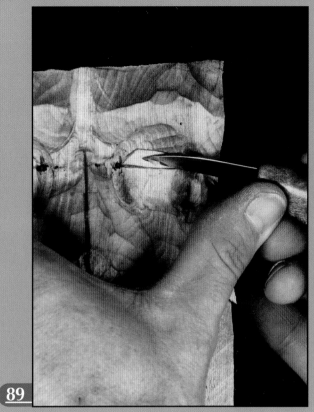

89

Continue to remove small slivers of wood.

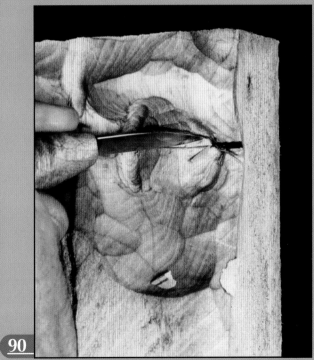

90

Clean up the outside corner with the point of your knife. This step is very important. These final cuts put the eyeball in the head at an anatomically correct angle. In Diagram 7 you can see how the eyeball cants at an inward angle from the top as it rests in the head.

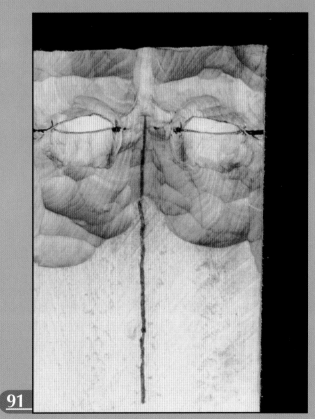

91

Both eyes are now complete.

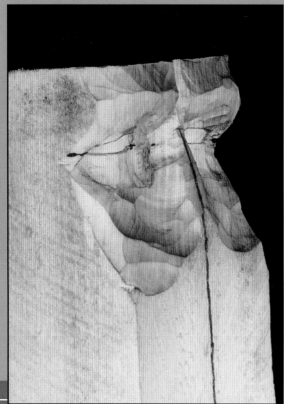

92

This three-quarter view clearly shows the thickness of the eyelids. Notice that they are not overly thick, but they are cleanly cut.

93

In this side profile view, you can easily see how the eyeball cants at an inward angle from top to bottom as it rests in the head.

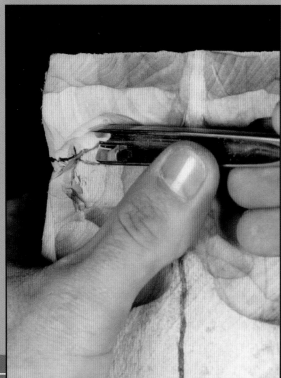

94

The next step is to set the area up for wrinkles in the eyelids and at the bottom of the eye. Using a #11 gouge, follow the shape of the eyeball and relieve a small amount of wood from the upper eyelid. Work from the center to the outside.

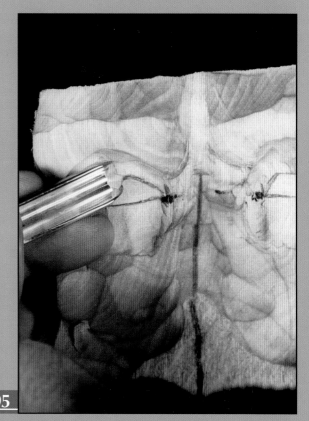

95

Reverse your cuts and work from the center to the inside. Keep in mind that you are relieving only a small amount of wood.

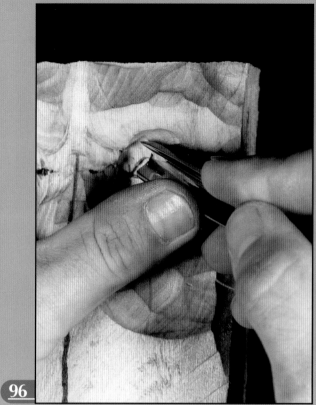

96 Make the same cuts on the right eye. Work from the outside to the inside first.

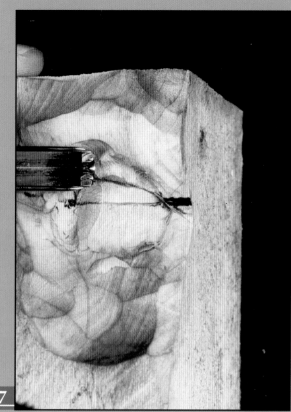

97 Reverse your cuts and work from the center to the outside.

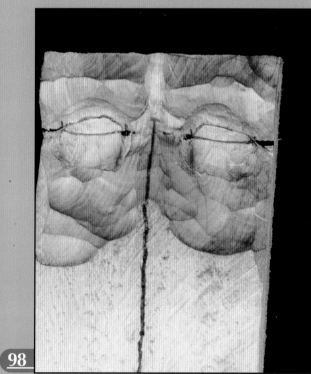

98 Here you can see the little gouge marks right above the contours of the top eyelid. This is where the wrinkle will fall on the top eyelid. The lower eyelid has what I call the basic three: three wrinkles in the bag area under the eye.

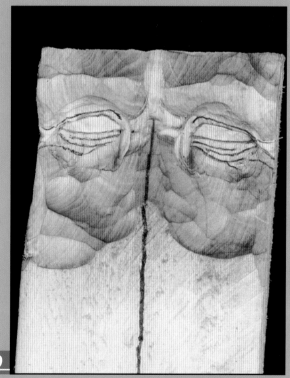

99 Draw in the wrinkles using Diagram 8 as a guide. These wrinkles are compression wrinkles. Because they happen in soft tissue, they will not be symmetrical from side to side.

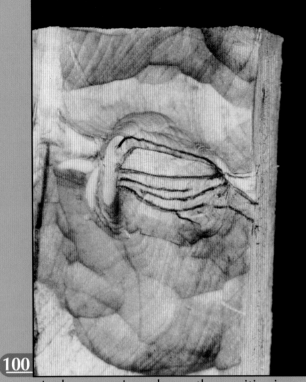

100

A close-up view shows the positioning of the wrinkles. Wrinkles tend to overlap each other on an imaginary centerline. They swing back and forth and often operate in a series of z's and y's.

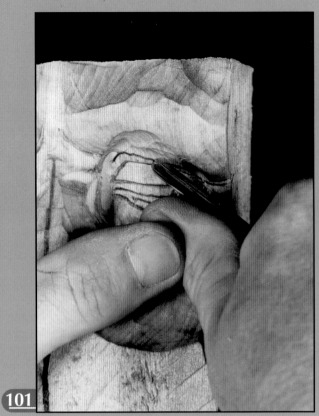

101

Use a V tool to carve the top wrinkle. Start at the center and work toward the inside corner.

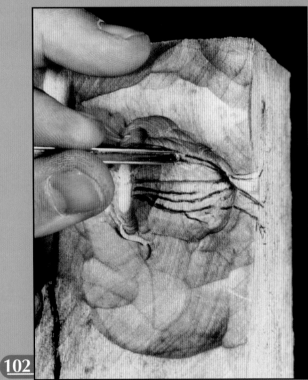

102

Finish the v-cut by working from the center to the outside corner. Making the v-cut in this manner will keep the eyelid from chipping off. Be sure that your tool is extremely sharp; otherwise the thin eyelid may crumble.

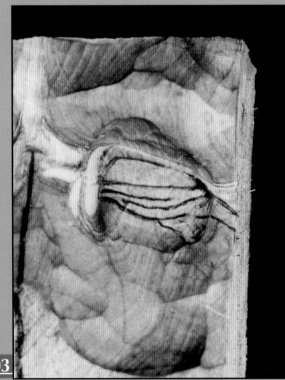

103

Here you can see the end result. Notice how the v-cut extends into the previously made gouge mark at the inside corner of the eye. It also extends into the cut previously made at the outside corner of the eye.

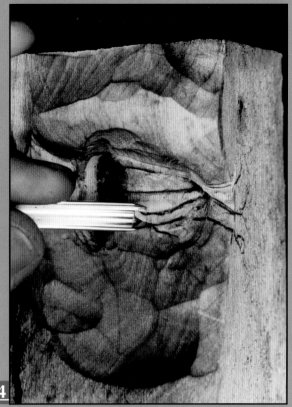

104

Using a #11 or #9 u-gouge, follow the wrinkle lines on the bottom of the eye.

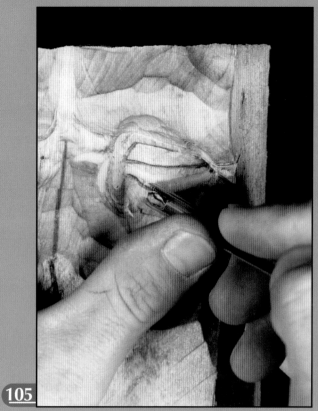

105

Cut from the center to the outside corners of the eye.

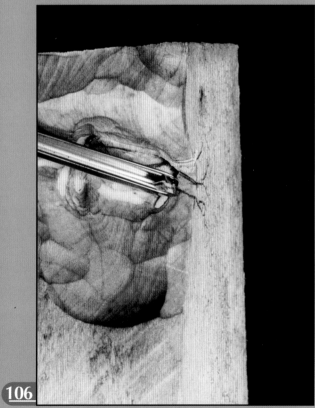

106

With a small u-gouge, cut in the crow's feet that wrap around the outside corner of the eye.

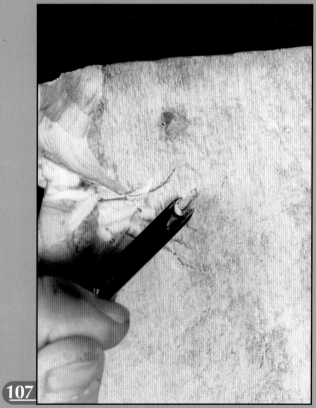

107

Continue to cut the wrinkles at the side of the eye. Notice how the wrinkles follow the anatomy of the face. The muscle and bone structure dictate where wrinkles can fall.

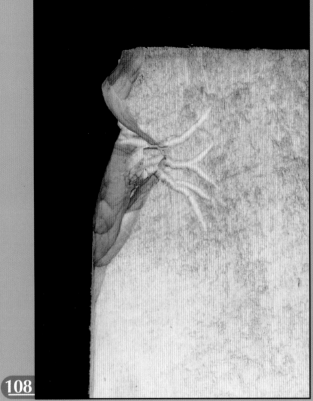

108

The completed crow's feet at the side of the eye should look like this.

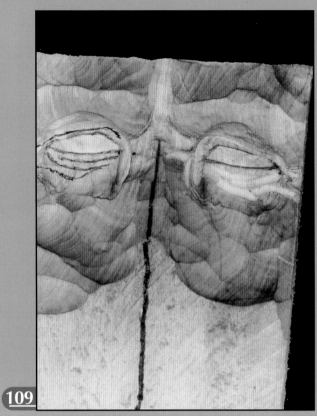

109

The wrinkles on the right side of the face have been cut in; the left side has yet to be done.

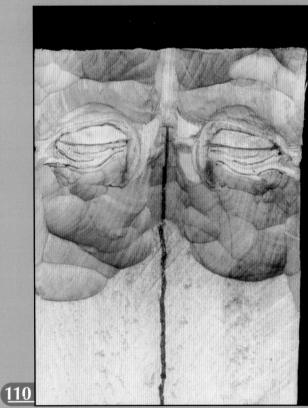

110

Cut the wrinkles on the left eye, then redraw the pencil lines down the middle of the gouge cut.

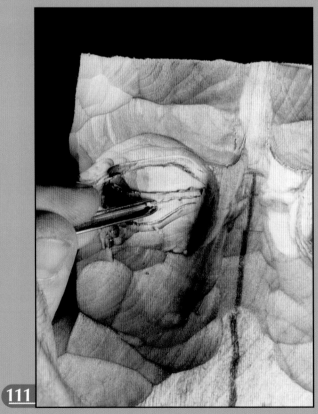

111

With a small v-tool, make a cut in the center of the u-gouge cut. This will sharpen the wrinkle and create the look of creased skin.

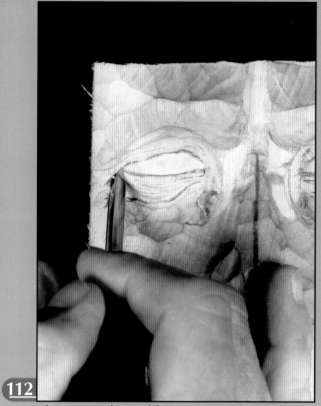

112

The second wrinkle carries right up to where the top eyelid overlaps the bottom eyelid.

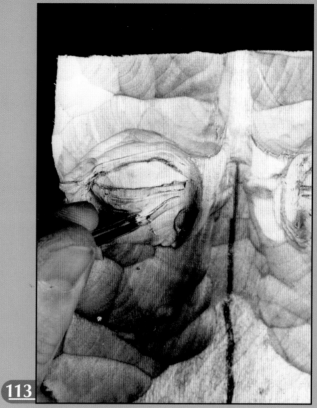

113

The last wrinkle runs from the left side of the eye to just shy of the inside corner.

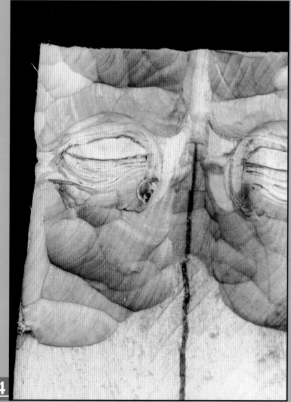

114

The wrinkles are completed.

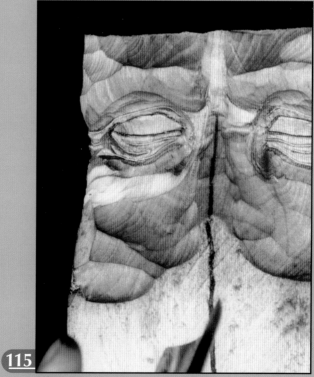

115

Use a big #7 gouge to remove a small amount of wood underneath the eye on the cheek area. This cut will set the cheek area back and create a smooth transition of form from the nose to the area underneath the eye on the front of the face.

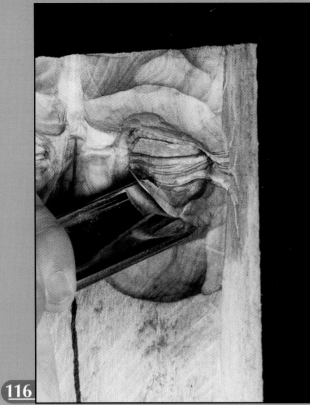

116

Make the same cut on the right side.

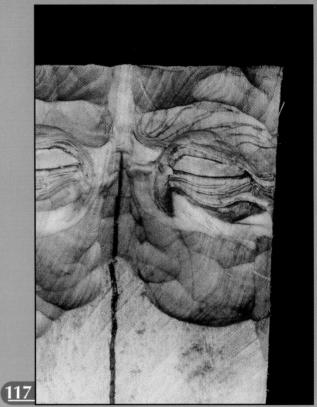

117

The light-colored wood shows where wood has been removed from the face. Draw in the eyebrows for reference. You are now ready to put the pupils in.

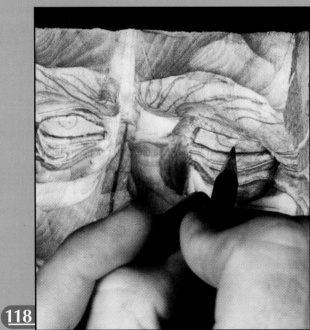

118

Draw in the pupils. This figure will have a "positive pupil." The pupil will be relieved by cutting away the iris. Refer to Diagram 8 in the back of this book. Notice that the pupils appear slightly off-center. Centered pupils are not natural and don't give the sculpture much life. Make sure, however, that both pupils are off-center in the same direction.

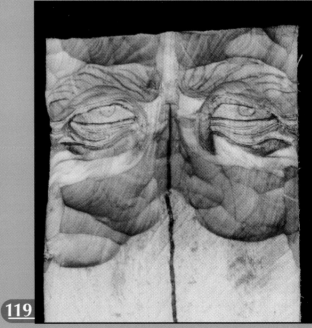

119

Here you can see the position of the eyebrows and the pupils. About one-third of the pupil is covered by the top eyelid, and about one-fourth of the iris is covered by the top eyelid.

34 • Carving Eyes

120

Use a #8 or #9 gouge between 3 mm and 5 mm wide depending on the size of the eye. Push the gouge in and rotate it, allowing the tool to slice its way around the pupil. I am using a #9 gouge in this photo.

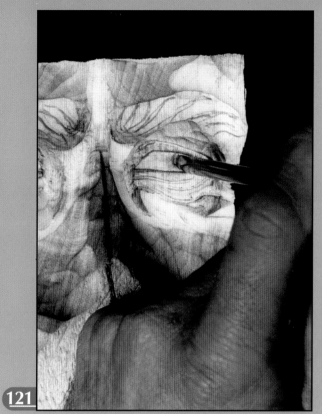

121

Make the same rotating cut on the right eye.

122

Using the same tool, mark the area for the iris. Come out just a couple millimeters from the pupil and make a stop cut. The iris touches the bottom eyelid or appears to be covered by just a small amount. Don't undercut the pupil or you will risk the popping out the pupil.

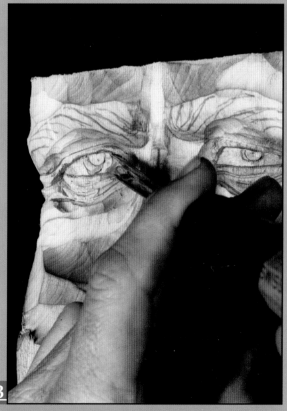

123

Make a second stop cut on the opposite side of the pupil.

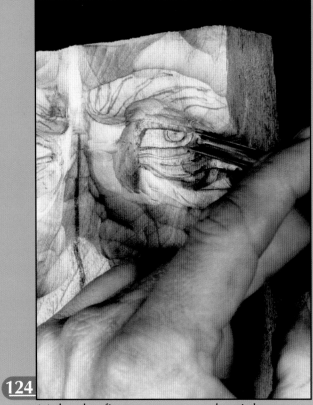

124

Make the first stop cut on the right eye…

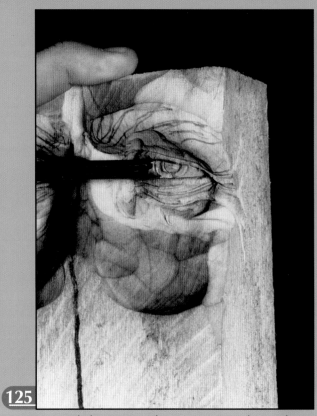

125

… and the second stop cut on the right eye.

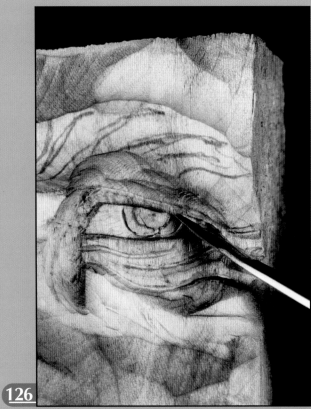

126

Insert your knife at the top of the iris and relieve that chip.

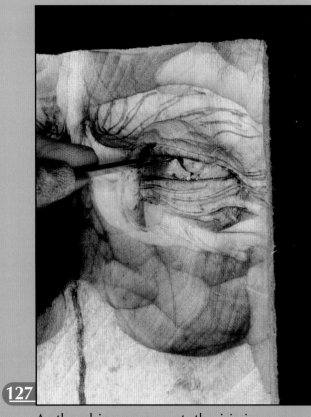

127

As the chips come out, the iris is recessed. The whites of the eye and the pupil are left proud.

The irises of both eyes have been removed.

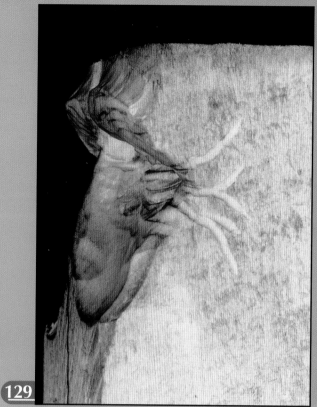

129
A side view shows the eye to this point. Again, notice how the brows protrude and how the eye cants at an inward and downward angle from the top.

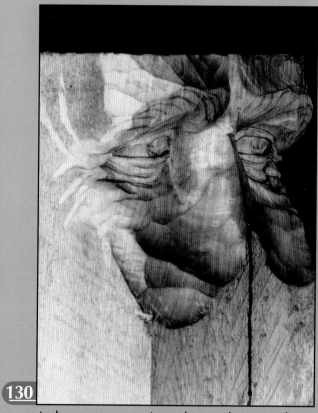

130
A three-quarter view shows the eyes from another angle.

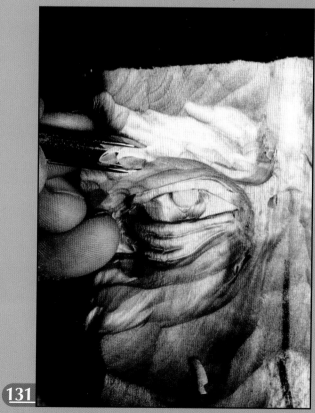

131
Use a #11 gouge to cut in the eyebrows. Work from the top in using short strokes.

Eye One

132

The first cuts of the eyebrow are complete.

133

Notice how the hair on the eyebrows follows the pattern of the eyebrow. Draw in a line to show the top edge of the eyebrow.

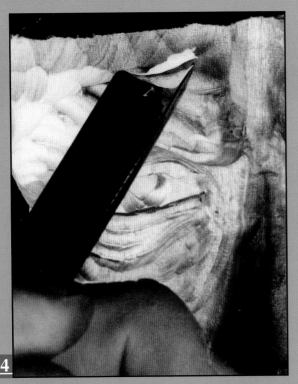

134

Using a #5 or #7 gouge, remove a little wood above the hair of the eyebrow. Slide the tool sideways, working from right to left, just above the top of the eyebrow where the hair ends.

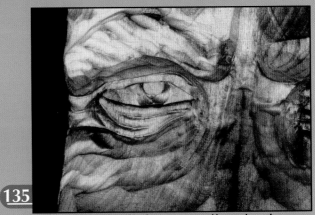

135

When finished, this cut will make the eyebrow protrude off the forehead just a little bit.

Moving On: Now that you've completed one eye, don't stop here. Keep practicing. A good way to practice eyes is to pick up a scrap piece of wood at the beginning of every carving session and carve an eye. If it looks nice, fine; if it doesn't look nice, fine. Don't run it in the ground or get yourself bored or frustrated. Just carve it, then toss it off to the side and go on to work on whatever else you had planned. At the end of a couple months, you'll be amazed at how much your eye carving skills have improved.

Eye Two: A Heavy-Lidded Eye

This next eye has a heavy lid on top. A bag on the top of the eye covers the top eyelid at the outside edge of the eye.

The pupil of this eye is often referred to as a "negative" pupil. To create it, the iris and the pupil are cut out. The whites of the eye are left as is. This type of eye works very well on smaller faces and figures. Once the wax and antiquing finish soak in, the effect is a very dramatic dark area suggesting the eye.

Before you begin, prepare a practice stick as instructed below. Practice sticks, or study sticks, are a great way to hone your carving skills. They are ideal for learning skills that a carver needs to repeat over and over to master.

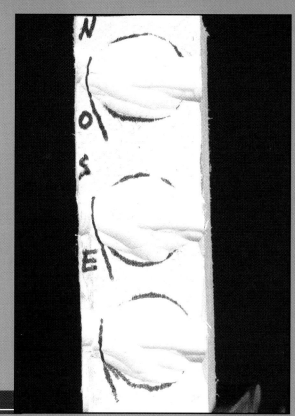

1 Mark three eyes on the face of the stick and carve the mound for each eye. (The steps to carve the mound are found in Eye One: Steps 1–23, Pages 5-10). Mark the nose side of the practice stick.

2 Use a #3, 1 in. gouge to soften up the corners of the block. Work the bottom corner and the top corner back.

3 Make the same cuts on the second and third eye. Note that the first and third eye have been done; I'm finishing up the cuts on the second eye.

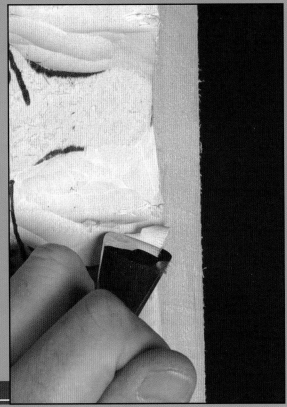

4

Work on knocking off the sharp edges. Clean up all three to keep each eye progressing at the same stage.

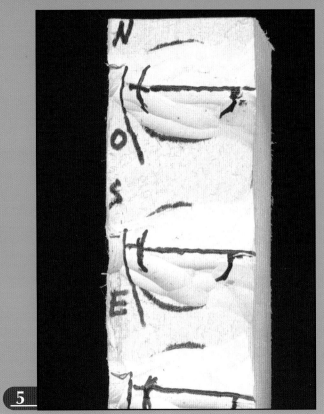

5

Draw in the half-circles that mark the edges of the eyeballs. Add the centerlines. You're now ready to carve the eye.

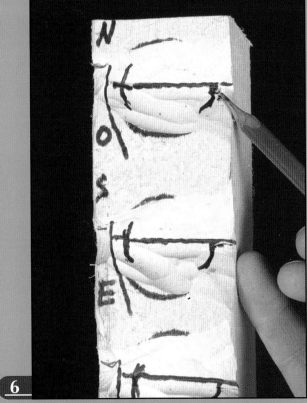

6

Notice how the mark for the mound stops at the centerline. This shorter mark leaves extra wood for the bag that hangs over the top eyelid.

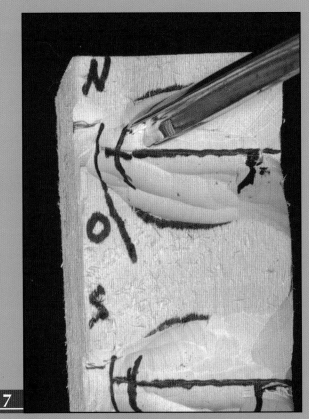

7

Begin your cuts at the inside corner. Cut from the top down to the center with a #11 gouge.

8 Cut up from the bottom to the center and relieve the chip.

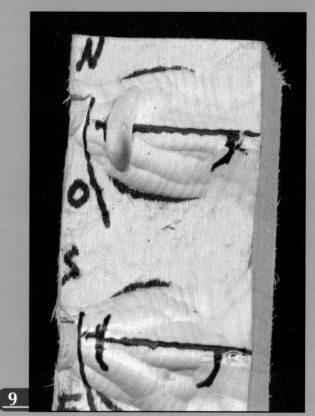

9 The cut is finished. Determine the size gouge you need based on the size of the eye that you are creating. Try to balance the eyeball in the socket. You don't want a gouge that cuts away too much of the eyeball and leaves a socket that's way too big.

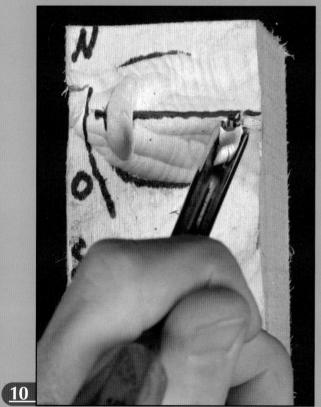

10 Move to the outside corner of the eye. Cut up to the centerline and stop.

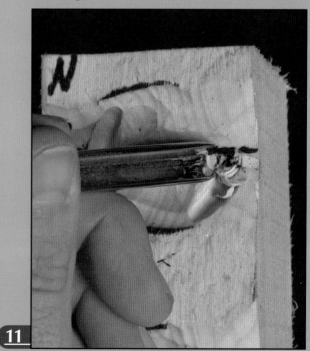

11 Relieve that chip right there at the center line.

12
A close-up view shows the finished cut. Notice how the top remains uncut. The extra wood above the centerline will be used for the heavy lid.

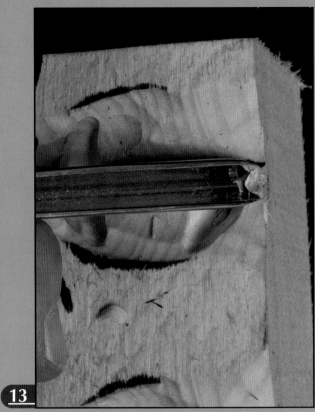

13
Using a #11 gouge, make a cut to the outside of the eye socket.

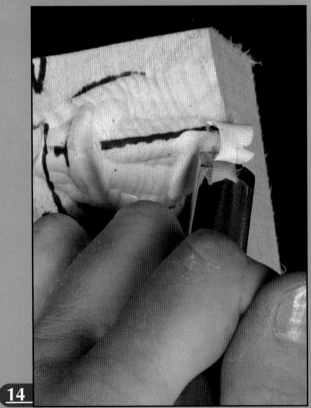

14
Using a #7 or #5, remove some wood to soften that outer bone around the eye.

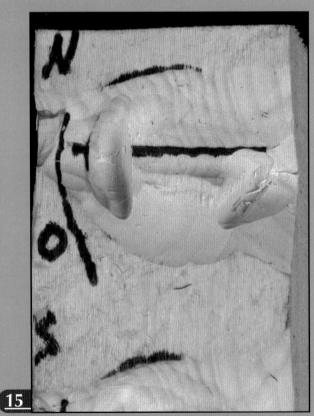

15
Here's what the cuts look like to this point.

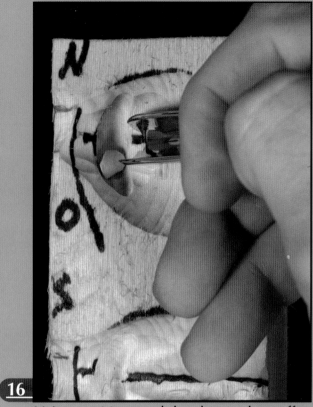

16

Using a #11, round the sharp edges off the inside corner of the eyeball. Strive to create a roundness from side to side, not up and down.

17

Round the outside corner of the eyeball below the centerline. Stay away from the top side of the eyeball.

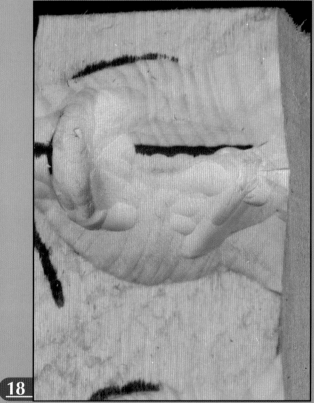

18

The rounding cuts are completed. Note how the sharp edges have been removed from the corners of the eyeball.

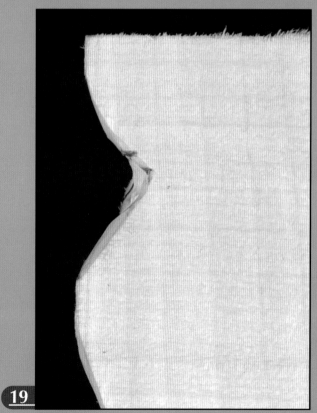

19

Study the side view. Notice how the orbit of the eye comes around the side of the face.

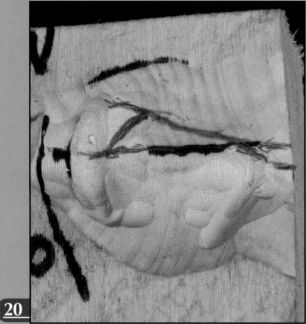

20

Redraw the centerlines. Extend those lines all the way to the edge of the block. This will provide a reference point. Draw in the slanting line for the bag. Redraw the curving line of the top eyelid. Note how this line stops at the slanting line of the bag. The heavy skin above the eye will cover part of the top eyelid.

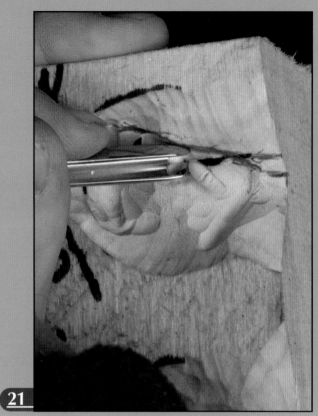

21

With a #11, relieve the wood underneath the bag line to show some definition. Cut from the inside out.

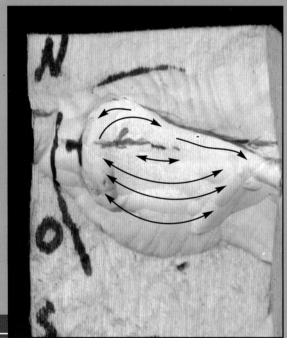

22

The next step is to recess the whole surface of that mound so that the entire mound is behind that sagging bag of skin on the upper part of the eye. As you can see by the arrows, you'll need to push the whole area back equally. Take small chips in the directions shown.

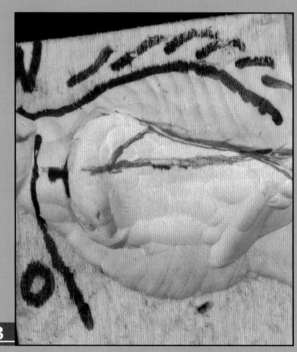

23

Redraw the centerline and the curving line of the top eyelid. Notice how the top eyelid disappears up and under the bag. Also notice how the bag of the eye extends down past the centerline and out over the side of the face.

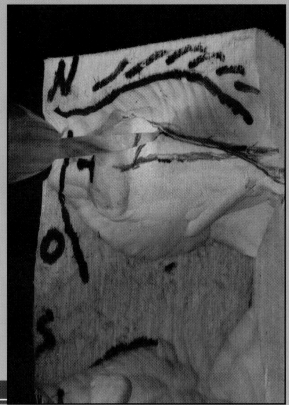

24 Using a very sharp carving knife, stop cut the curving line of the upper eyelid.

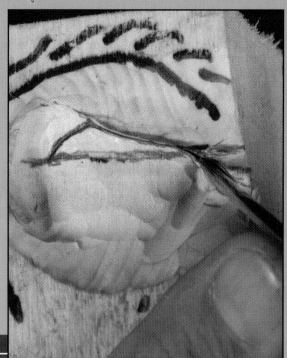

25 Make a second stop cut along the bag line. Start this stop cut at the intersection of the stop cut you made in Step 18 and the bag line. Carry it down through the deep spot in the corner of the eye and right on out the corner of the block.

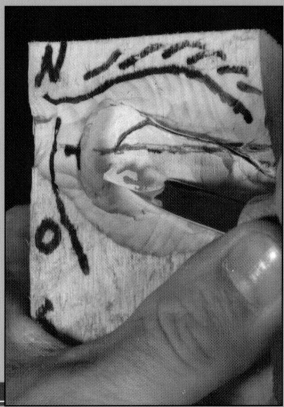

26 Using the knife and starting low on the eyeball, cut in and straight up to the stop cuts. Remove just a very thin shaving. You can see by the photo that the piece of wood being removed is not very thick.

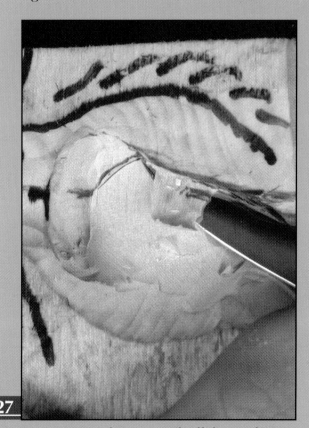

27 Continue to shave wood off the surface of the eyeball. Maintain the roundness that was already established and cut only up to the stop cut.

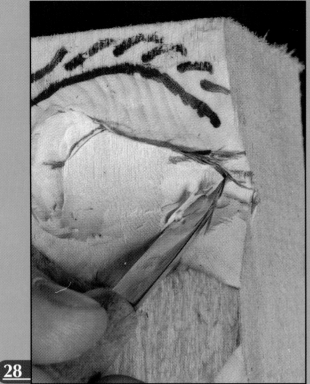

28

This tricky little cut will deepen the outside corner of the eye and help to maintain the eye's roundness. Start here at the corner of the eye, the curl the knife right around...

29

...until the cut stops at the stop cut of the upper eyelid.

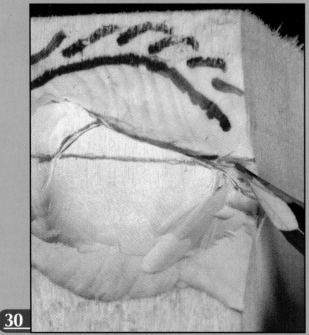

30

Redraw the centerline using the two remaining parts of the line as reference points. Notice how the small shavings have rounded the surface of the eye and relieved the eyelid just slightly.

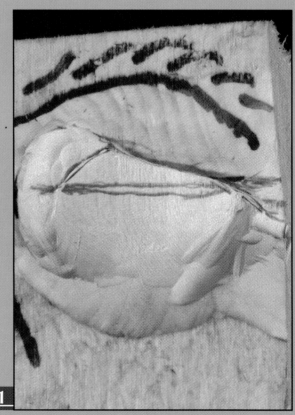

31

Draw in a bottom eyelid. The bottom eyelid is very close to the centerline and does not drop down very far.

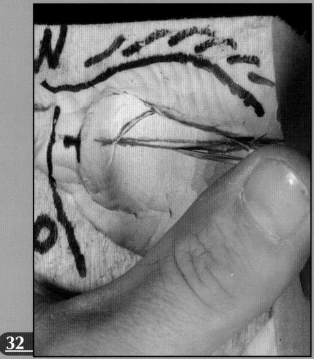

32

Make a stop cut along the bottom eyelid. and now we have to relieve it. From here on out, never cut up again, never. I can't stress this enough.

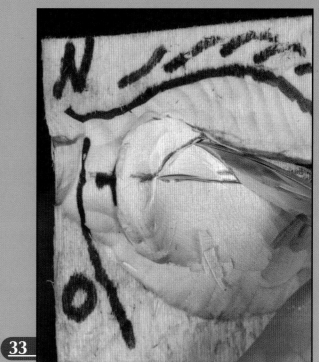

33

The next step is to relieve the bottom eyelid. During this process, never cut up. Cutting up will push the eye backwards in the head and give it an unnatural look. Starting at the top eyelid, shave down to the bottom eyelid and recess the eyeball.

34

Work into the corner, always cutting down. A 1 mm or 2 mm skew chisel is an ideal tool for this tiny area.

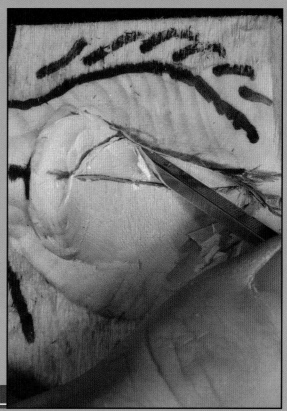

35

Continue working with the skew chisel to remove the wood that will relieve the lower eyelid.

Eye Two

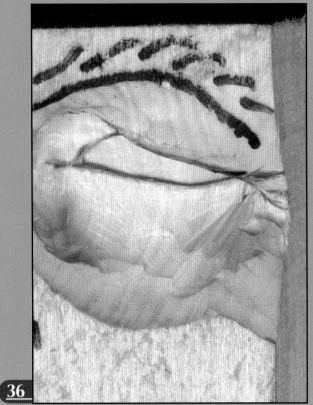

36

The bottom eyelid has been relieved. Notice how the bag hangs down over the top eyelid.

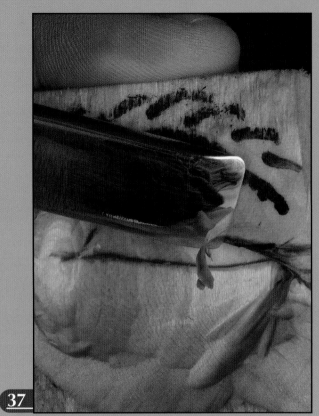

37

Turn a #5 gouge upside-down. Soften the sharp edge on the edge of the bag. You want this area to look like a fold of skin, not a sharp, square cut.

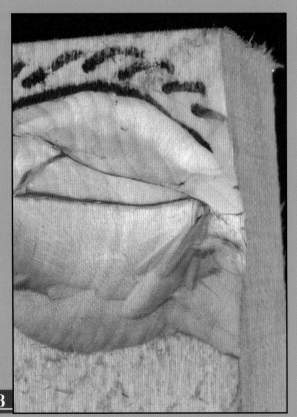

38

Notice how the cut from the previous step removed the pencil line and softened the bag. Now what we have to do is go in and deepen the inside corner around the eye opening.

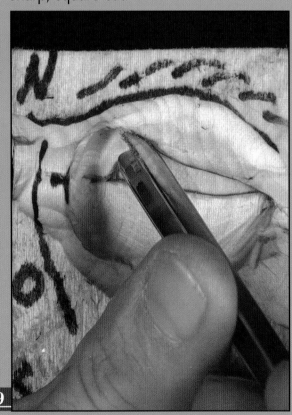

39

Use a #11, 3 mm gouge to make the inside corner deeper. Start at the inner part of the eye where the bag of the eye blends up into the brow.

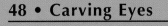

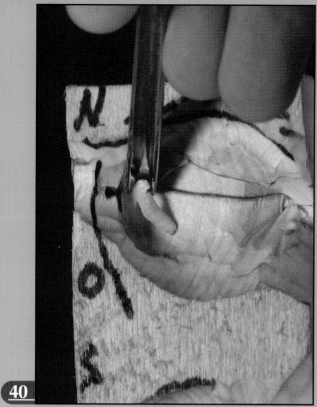

40

Cut inward and downward, following the curve of the eye. The cut ends here.

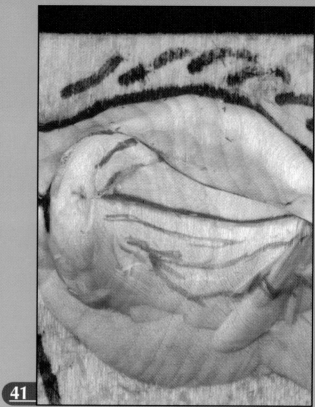

41

Draw a wrinkle on the top eyelid and the three basic wrinkles on the bottom of the eye. Refer to the diagrams at the back of this book for placement.

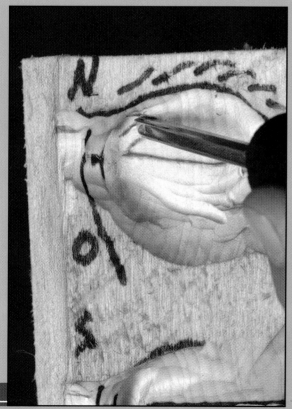

42

Using a very small v-tool, cut in the little wrinkle on the top eyelid. Then, cut in the wrinkles on the bottom of the eye with a small u-gouge.

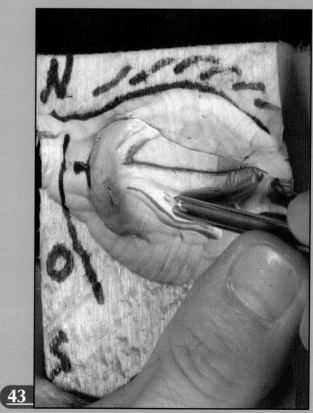

43

Sharpen the wrinkles by cutting into the bottom of the u-gouge cuts with a v-tool.

44

Take a few minutes to study the eye before moving on to cut in the pupil. Your carved eye should match the eye in this photograph.

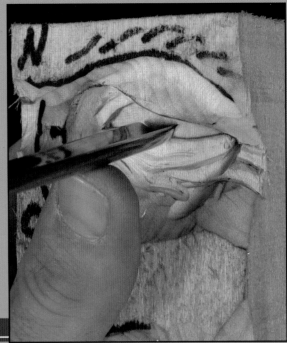

45

Use a #7, 4 mm gouge. This cut is "tool specific." The tool creates the exact size and shape of cut that you need. Push the tool in at the bottom eyelid. Rotate the tool as you push it in. Let the tool slice its way through the wood; don't force it. Your tool needs to be extremely sharp for this step.

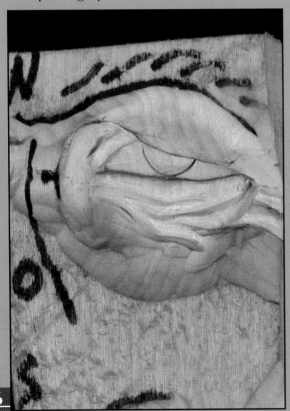

46

The pupil is cut in. Notice how the curve of the tool has made a perfect circle for the eye.

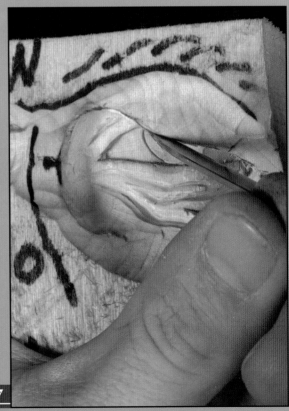

47

The next step is to remove that chip of wood. Cut in here where the gouge cut meets the drooping bag. Make a good, strong cut.

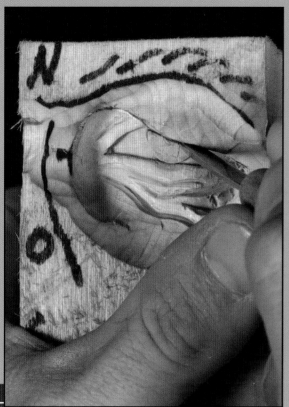

48 Continue the cut to the edge of the pupil. Notice how the chip is starting to come out.

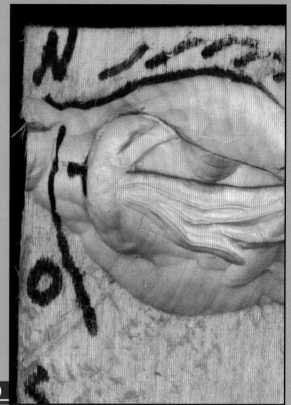

49 The eye is complete. Notice the drooping bag that appears to cover the top eyelid, the wrinkles and the recessed negative eye

Moving On: Use a practice stick to perfect your eye-carving skills. Create the mounds for several eyes on one practice stick. Then repeat the same cuts for each eye as you work your way down the stick. Repetition is the best way to learn a new skill. It helps you to fully understand the cuts and it helps you to build confidence in your new-found skill. Even experienced carvers like me find this technique useful to "warm up" before carving the eyes on a commission or other important piece.

Eye Three: A Baggy Eye

This third eye has a heavy top eyelid, a heavy bottom eyelid and a heavy bag under the eye. This type of eye would be used on an aged figure who has spent a lot of time in the elements. Native American elders, old frontiersmen and weathered sea captains are good example of figures that might have this type of an eye.

As with all of the other sample eyes, you will need to create a socket and a mound; but then you'll be doing a few things differently.

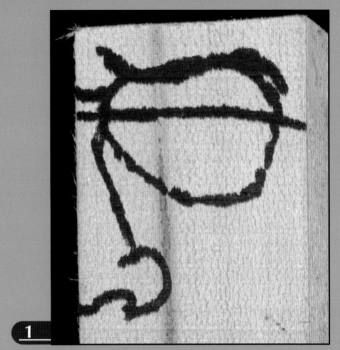

1

Roughly draw the socket shape and lines to indicate the nose, the brow bone and the den in the nose, which is above the centerline. (You can lay a pencil right in that dent in your nose and look right under it. That's what tells me that the center of the actual eye opening i just a little below that dent.)

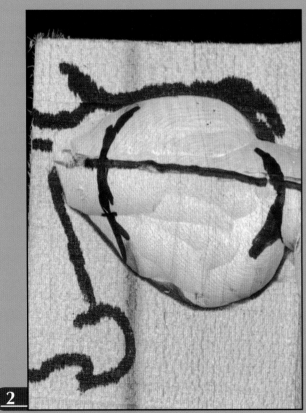

2

Create the socket with a #11 gouge. Redraw the centerline and add marks to indicate the edges of the eyes.

3

Number 11 gouges are essential for doing eyes because they give you a nice deep u-shaped cut. Cut from the top down on the inside of the eye.

4 Cut from the bottom up on the outside of the eye.

5 Cut up to the center line. Leave the chip in place. Then start at the top and cut down to the center line. The chip should fall out clean.

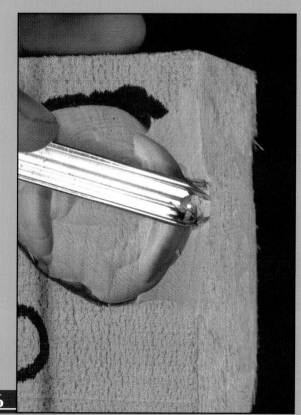

6 Cut the outside orbit of the eye. Don't be afraid to push the tool into the wood.

7 Round off the sharp edge on the inside corner of the eye. This area of the eye is shaped like half of a cylinder or, as a more common reference, half of a soda can sitting vertically in the socket.

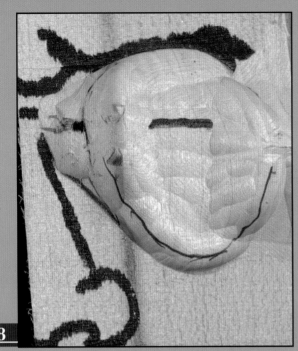

8

Round off the sharp edge on the outside corner of the eye to complete the half-cylinder shape. Don't cut too much of the center line away or you may lose the half-cylinder shape. Draw a line that shows how low the bag will fall.

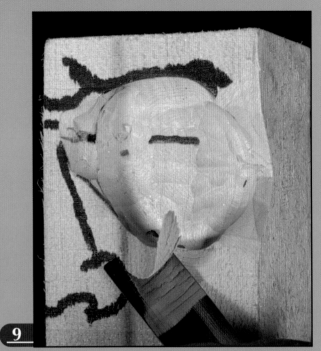

9

Carve away the heavy ridge that's left under the eye with a #5 gouge. This is the surface of the front of the cheek and it needs to be pushed back almost flush with the gouge. Cut around the bottom of the socket. Start in the middle and work up to the side of the nose using the corner of the gouge.

10

Come back to the middle and work up toward the outside of the eye.

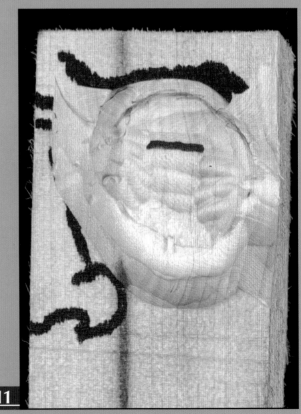

11

With a deep #11 gouge, make a gouge cut at the inside edge of the previous cut. This cut will start to bring the bag out.

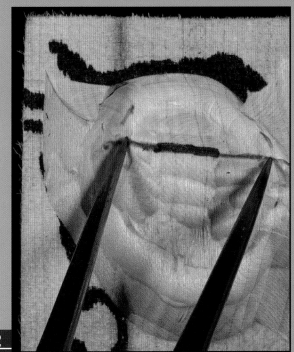

12

Redraw the center line. With a pair of calipers, measure the width of the eye opening. Notice where the eye opening starts and stops. It doesn't start right up against the nose; it's actually in that u-gouge cut you made when you created the mound.

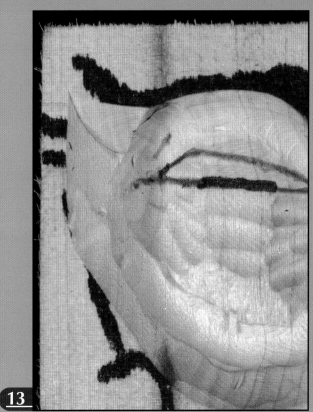

13

Draw in the top eyelid using the caliper measurements as a guide. Be sure to continue the line for the top eyelid down and off the outside corner of the eye.

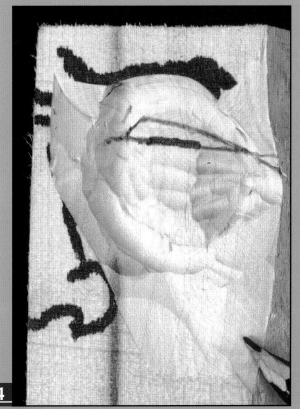

14

Take some more wood off the cheek area underneath the bag. Push that entire area back so that the lower part of that bag protrudes a little bit.

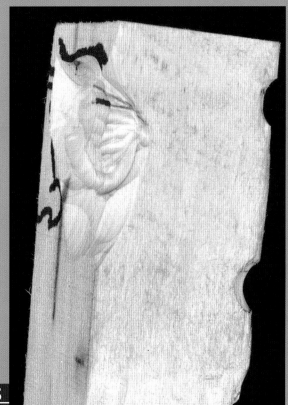

15

Here's a side view of the same area. Notice how the cheek area is pushed back behind the bag area.

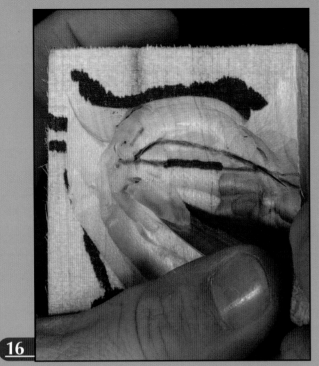

16

Cut across the top of the upper eyelid with a gouge to deepen this area. Make a stop cut along the upper eyelid; then start at the bottom of the eye and cut up to the stop cut at the upper eyelid.

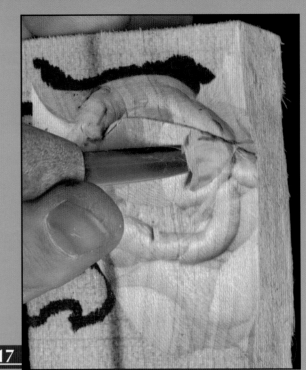

17

Cut in at the outside corner and turn the knife so that it cuts a chip away from the corner and deepens this area. Notice how heavy the top eyelid looks due to the u-gouge cut made in the previous step.

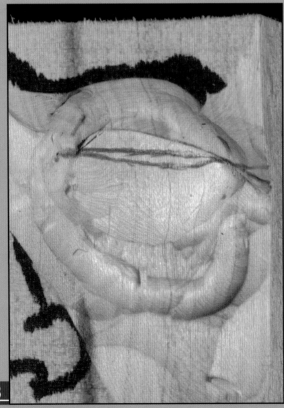

18

Redraw the centerline. Draw in the bottom eyelid.

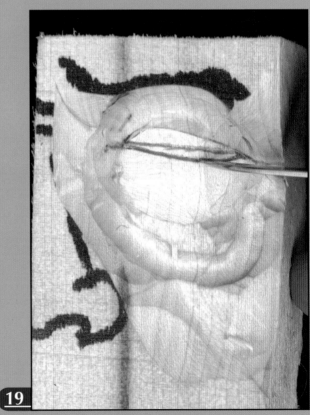

19

With a sharp carving knife, make a stop cut along the line for the bottom eyelid.

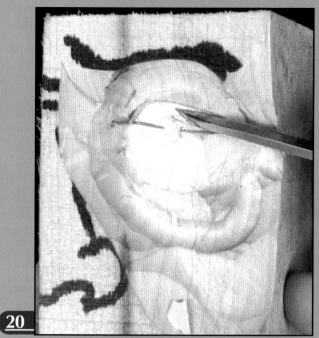

20

Using a small skew chisel, cut down from the top eyelid to the bottom eyelid. Strive to relieve the top eyelid just a bit. Remember to always cut from the top eyelid down; never from the bottom eyelid up. This process automatically sets the eye in the head at an anatomically correct angle.

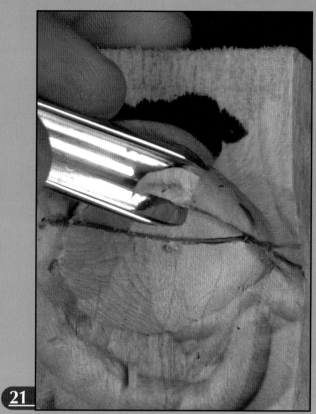

21

Cut across the top eyelid with a deep #11 gouge. Your goal is to contour the eyeball shape all the way across.

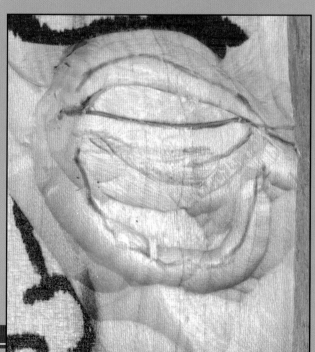

22

Up until this point, the creation of this eye has been similar to that of the Eye One and Eye Two. Now the process changes. Draw in the wrinkles. The wrinkle on top and the wrinkle on the bottom will be very deep. Refer ahead to Step 37 to see the shape of the bag and the depth of the wrinkles.

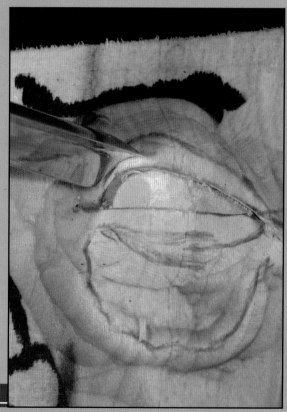

23

Using a #7 gouge, start the cuts above the eyelid. Try to maintain the curve of the eyelid and the distance between the bottom of the gouge and the edge of the top eyelid.

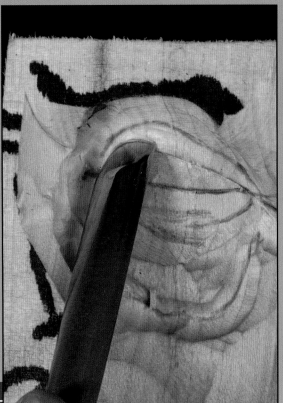

24

The first third of the inside of the eye has more of an arch, so a #7 gouge is required. Push the gouge straight up into the wood.

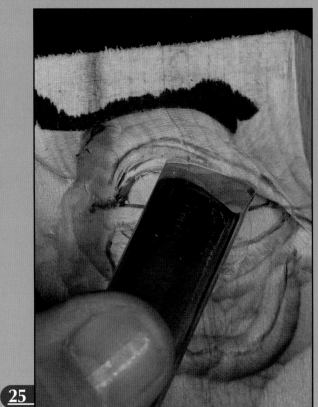

25

Switch to a #5 gouge of the same width for the remainder of the eyelid cuts. Continue to follow the contour of the eyeball so that the cuts follow the shape of the eyeball.

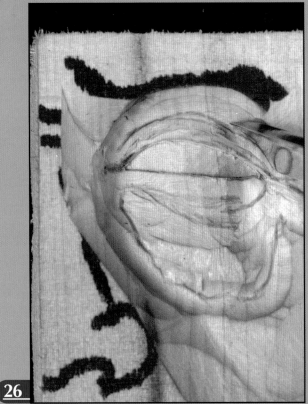

26

Cut straight in with a #5 chisel all the way along the contour of the eye to relieve the chip.

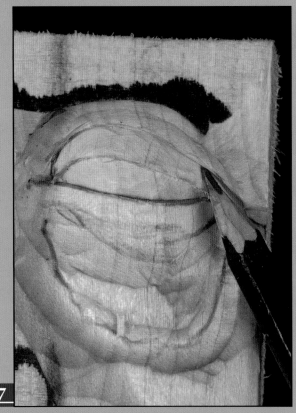

27

This photo shows the finished result. You may want to repeat this process a couple times to achieve the appropriate depth.

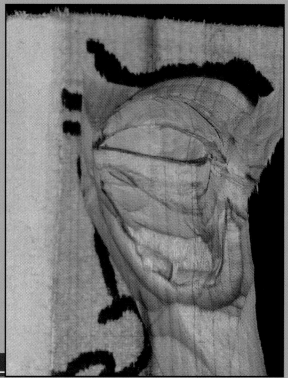

28 If you have done the previous steps correctly, these cuts will make the eyelid appear to be round on top. Here you can see that a little bit better. Notice how the cuts have made the lid appear very, very heavy.

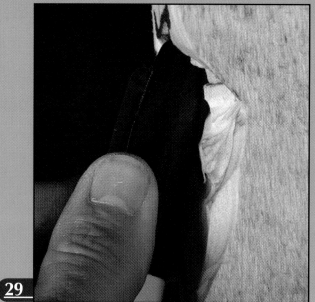

29 A side view shows the progress to this point. Notice the little indentation just below the bottom eyelid. As the face ages, the heavy skin below the eye falls due to gravity and time. The eyelids, however, contain little strips of cartilage that help them to hold their shape. Because of this, the eyelid must be carved to make it appear to contour the eyeball.

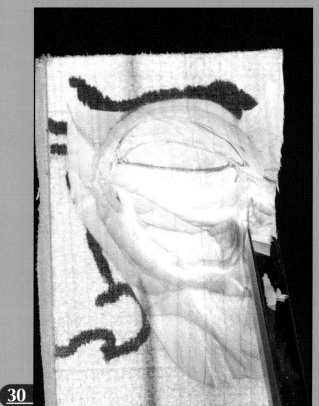

30 Using a #11 u-gouge, carve in the two deep wrinkles under the eye. Push the face down around that big bag with a #5 or #7.

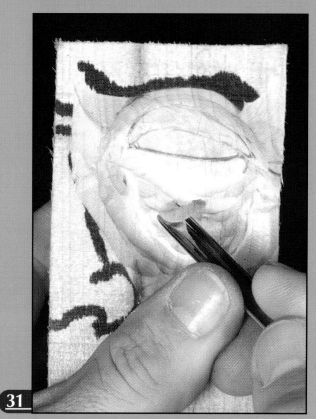

31 Refine some of the wrinkles on the heavier mass of baggy skin that hangs below the eye with a #11 gouge.

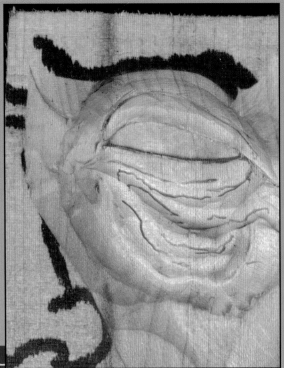

32

Draw in the smaller wrinkles with a pencil. Notice how the ends of my pencil marks tend to overlap from wrinkle to wrinkle. These "compression" wrinkles appear when gravity and age take their toll on a face.

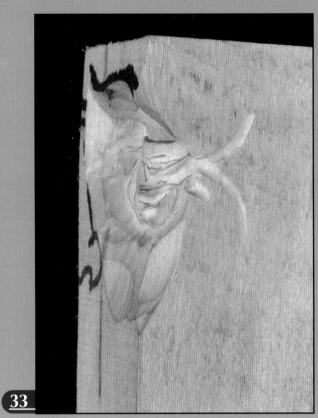

33

A side view shows how the wrinkles and crow's fee continue off the side of the face.

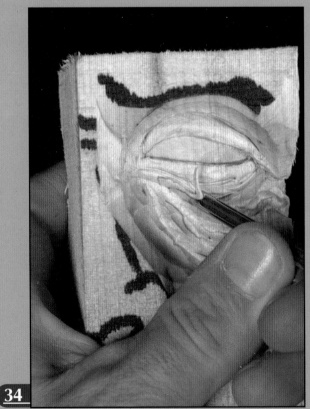

34

As before, use a u-gouge to make the initial cut of the wrinkle...

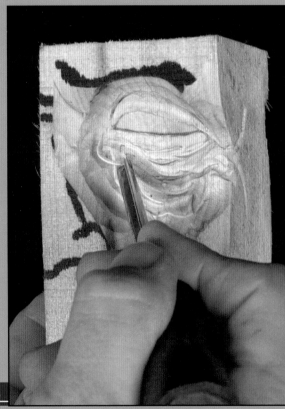

35

... then use a v-tool along the bottom of the u-gouge cut to sharpen the wrinkle.

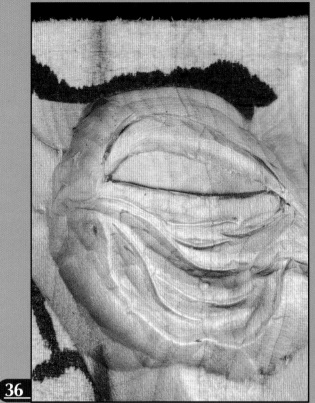

36

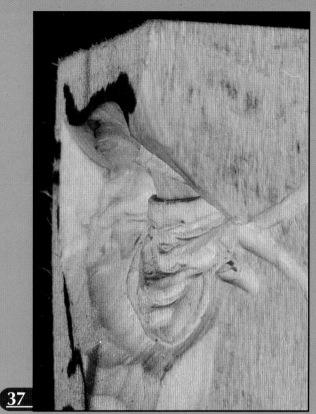

37

A close-up of the finished eye. Notice the beginnings of the smooth transition into the cheek and nose areas.

A side view gives a better look at how the wrinkles extend around the side of the face. Notice the inward and downward angle of the eyeball. Also take note of how the bag appears to be on top of the face due to its puffy nature. Use the type of pupil you would like, put it in and finish it.

Moving On: Try making a study stick to remind you of the steps you used to carve a certain type of eye. A study stick is different from a practice stick in that the study stick shows the progression of the carving. At the top of the study stick, carve the mound. Move down the stick and carve the mound plus the next several steps. Move down the stick and carve the mound plus the steps from the previous eye plus the next several steps. Continue in this manner until you have a study stick that will remind you how to carve that particular eye.

Eye Four: A Winking Eye

This fourth eye is a winking eye. It is a study in muscle structure and the creation of wrinkles. This type of eye can be used on any figure.

As with all of the other sample eyes, you will need to create a socket and a mound; however, because this eye has a different overall shape, the creation is a bit different.

1

Draw the outline of the eye's shape and lines to indicate the nose and brow placement. Notice that the winking eye takes on more of a football shape. The angles of the deepened areas on the outside and inside corners of the eye are much more extreme than the previous sample eyes.

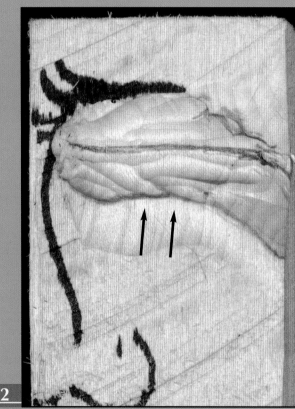

2

Using a #11 gouge, create the socket. The arrows and the dashed line show how the muscles of the eye push the face and the eye up into almost an S-shaped curve. Look in the mirror and wink at yourself to get a better idea of this effect. Redraw the centerline.

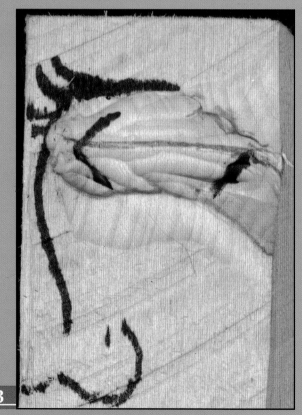

3

Draw in the outlines of the mound. Even though there is no eye visible, the mound is still an important structure and needs to be carved first.

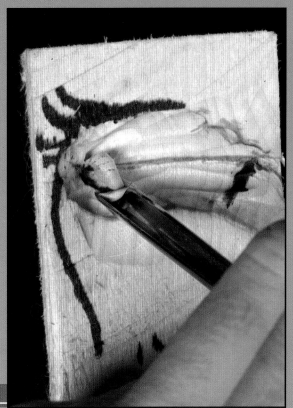

4 Cut down to the centerline on the inside corner of the eye with the #11 gouge, leaving the chip in place; then cut up to the centerline. The chip will pop out.

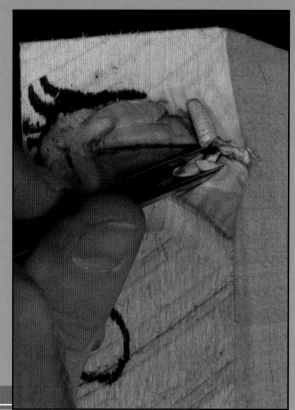

5 Still using the #11 gouge, deepen the outside corner of the eye. First, cut up to the centerline, stop, then trim out the chips.

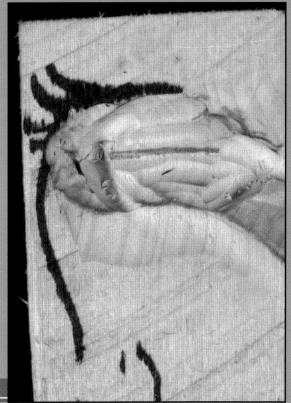

6 Then cut through to the outside corner of the eye. If you're following these demonstrations in order, you'll notice that the top cut on the outside corner of the eye has been omitted.

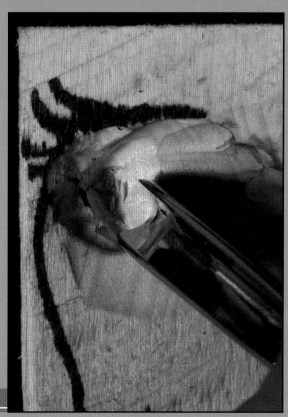

7 Round off the sharp edges with a #11 or a #9 gouge. Chose the gouge that best fits the size of the eye.

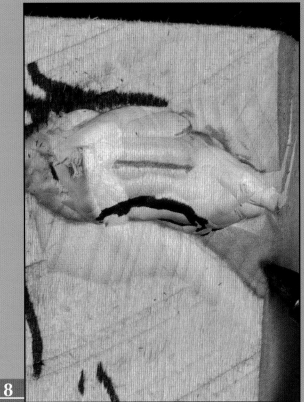

8

The mound has been roughed in. The black marker line at the bottom of the eye indicates the area where the facial muscles will "scrunch up" the winking eye.

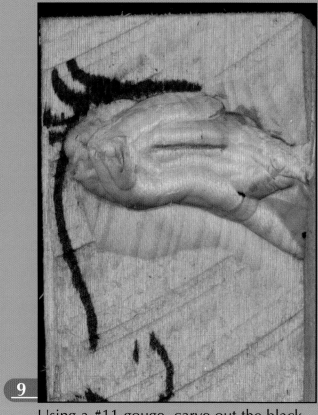

9

Using a #11 gouge, carve out the black marker line to shape and deepen this area.

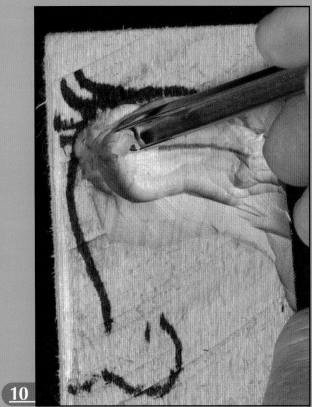

10

Still using the #11 gouge, clean out and deepen the inside corner a bit. Keep your centerline in place at all times: Do not carve it away.

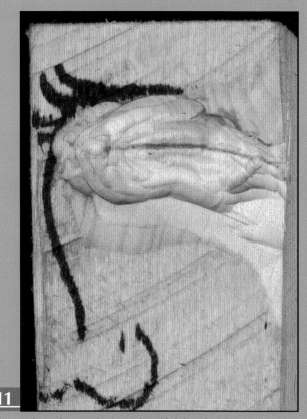

11

The shaped eye should look like this. The edges have been rounded and the corners cleaned up. You'll also want to soften the area where the eye meets the cheek.

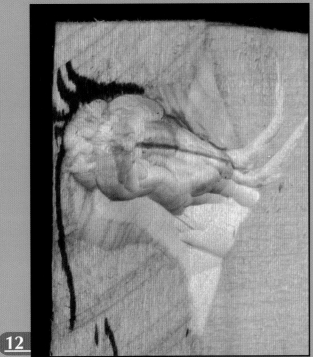

12

The mound is clearly visible in this side view. Notice that the mound is quite a bit narrower than that of an open eye. Of course, you still have to create the proper structure and the proper look and the proper mass to make the wink look realistic.

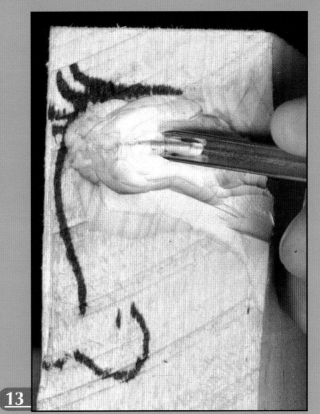

13

Using a #11 gouge, cut straight across the center line where the eyelids meet.

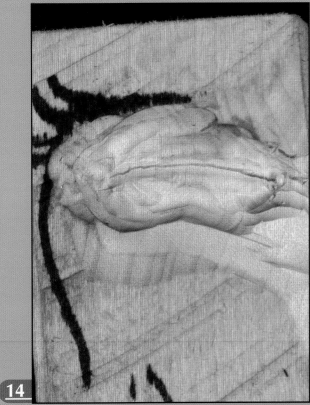

14

Redraw the centerline all the way across the eye.

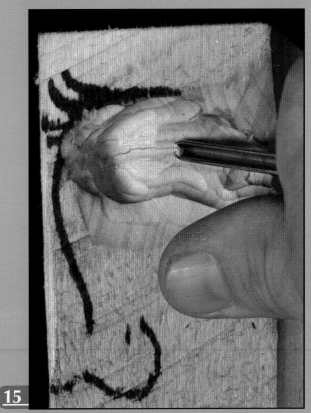

15

Cut right along that centerline again, this time with a tiny v-tool. This cut will make a slight arch.

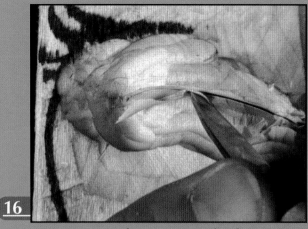

16 Using a very sharp carving knife, cut a stop cut along the bottom of the v-cut. Cut in again and remove a sliver of wood from the bottom side. Notice that the sliver of wood coming out of the crease is very thin.

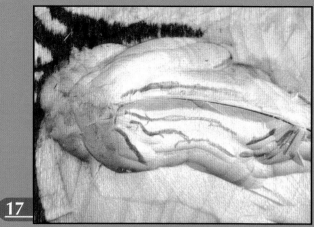

17 The separation between the top and bottom eyelids is complete. Draw in additional wrinkles. Notice how the wrinkle pattern changes for a winking eye. The wrinkles rise in the center as opposed to blending in on down the face.

18 Define the top eyelid with a v-gouge. Carve the wrinkles on the bottom eyelid with a u-gouge. Then sharpen the wrinkles by cutting into each u-gouge cut with a v tool. Stay away from the opening where the eyelids meet.

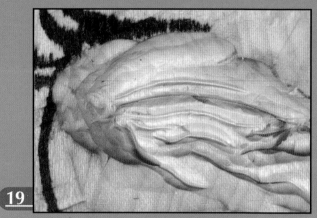

19 A close-up gives you a good look at the finished wrinkles. You can clearly see where the muscles have "scrunched up" the wrinkles in the center of the eye.

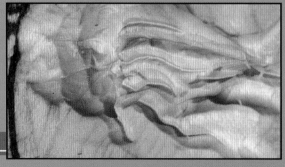

20 A three-quarter view gives you another look at the finished winking eye. Notice how the mound is still visible underneath all those wrinkles.

Moving On: If carving eyes is a skill you want to master, create a notebook or file of examples of various eyes. Cut photographs out of magazines, take pictures of other sculptures, ask a friend to pose for you while you make sketches of different eye expressions…. All of this research will help you to understand the eye and the muscle structures beneath it.

Eye Five: A Sleeping Eye

The last eye to be demonstrated is a sleeping, or closed, eye. This eye is relatively easy, but just because it is easier doesn't mean that the basics are unimportant. It is still imperative that you start with a properly structured mound and that you are precise in locating the nose and the brow.

This eye can also be used on any figure. It is an ideal eye to use if you are unsure of your skills at carving an open eye. Be sure to match all of the other features to the eye: A sleeping eye calls for a face that is also at rest.

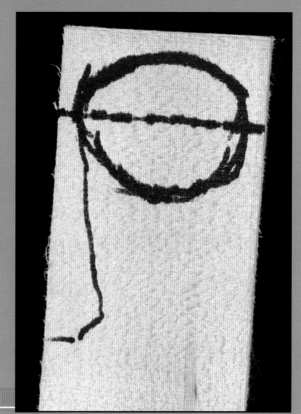

1

Sketch the eye on a block of wood. Draw in the centerline.

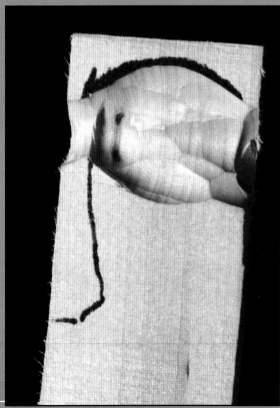

2

Using a #9 gouge, create the socket. On a practice block like this one, the socket should be approximately ¼ inch deep. Cut in, just a bit, at the outside and inside corners.

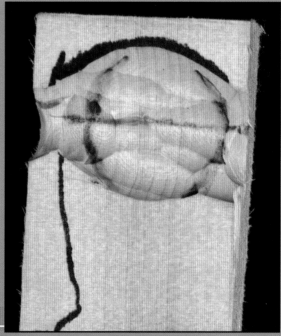

3

Redraw the centerline and sketch in the brow line. Also draw in the two semi-circular guidelines for the mound. Notice that the mound is quite bigger and rounder because there's no muscle action happening: no squinting or contracting of the muscles around the eye. The top eyelid just... falls

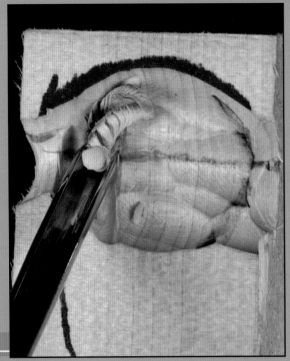

4

Cut in from the bottom up to the center and down from the top to the center with a #11 gouge. The cuts meet in the middle. Notice that no wood is being removed from the center part of the mound.

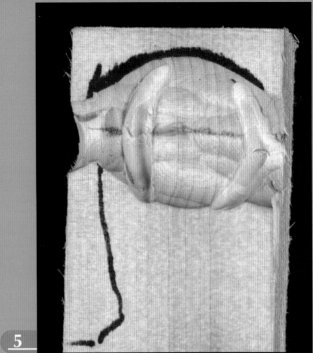

5

Repeat the same process on the outside corner of the eye. Make the small cut from the outside corner of the eye to the side of the face. This small cut around the to the corner of the face allows the viewer to see the eye from the side of the face.

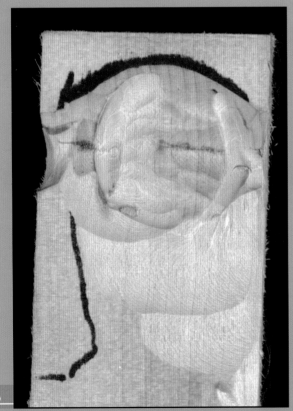

6

Round the mound. In this photo, the left side is rounded; the right side has yet to be done. Remove some wood underneath the eye to begin that smooth transition from the side of the nose to the eye area.

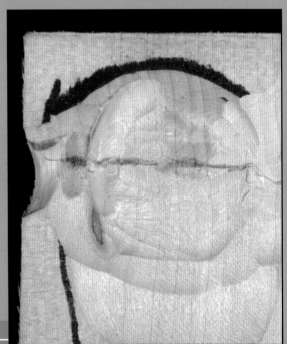

7

Continue to round the mound. Round off both corners so that the mound is rounded from side to side. Clean off the outer brow and the outer cheek bone area. Remove a small amount of wood from below the centerline to push the bottom of the eye back just a bit. Redraw the center line.

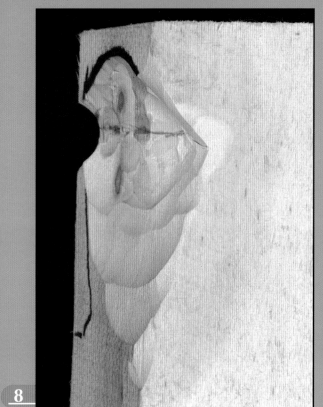

8

A side view shows the cuts from a different angle. Even though the eye is closed, notice how the eye still tilts inward, from top to bottom, in the face.

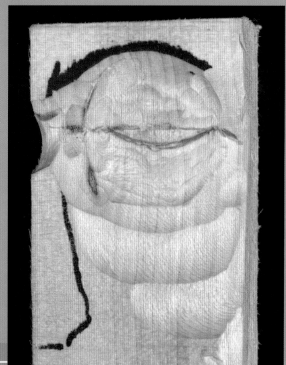

9

Draw in the line where the top and bottom eyelid meet. Notice that this meeting point is below the center line. The top eyelid comes down to meet the bottom eyelid and therefore has an upward arch, like a smile.

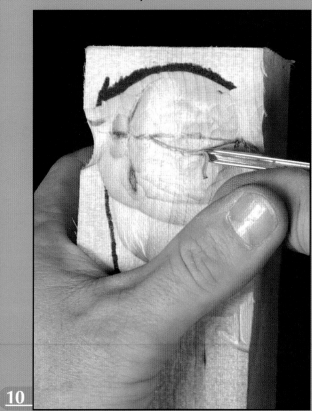

10

Using a sharply angled, small v-tool, make a v-cut along the line where the eyelids meet.

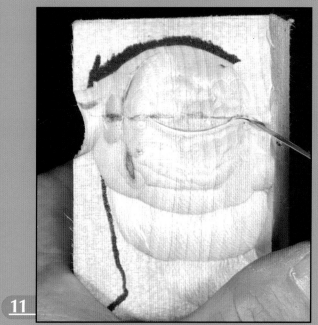

11

Using a very sharp carving knife, make a stop cut along the line where the lids meet. Continue this cut to the outside corner of the block. Note that even though the eye is closed, the separation between the top and the bottom eyelids is fairly sharp. Also, the fact that the bottom eyelid tucks under the top eyelid needs to be taken into consideration.

Eye Five

Carving Eyes • 69

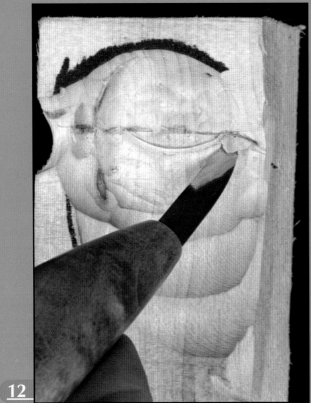

12

Still using the carving knife, take a small chip of wood out of the outside corner of the eye to show how the bottom eyelid tucks up underneath the top eyelid.

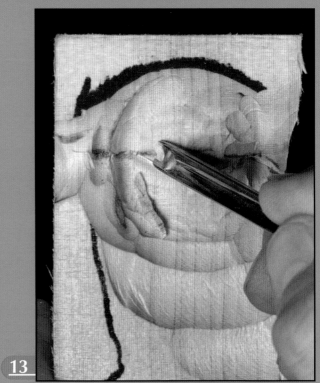

13

Instead of wrinkles, the cartilage is visible in the bottom and the top eyelids of a sleeping eye. Use a #9 gouge to make a slight cut right along the top side of the line where the eyelids meet.

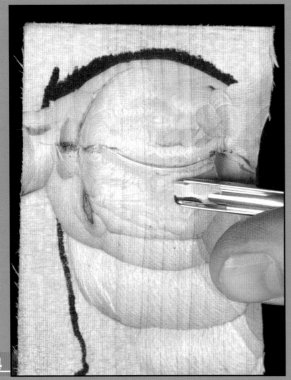

14

Make the same cut on the bottom eyelid. For reference, feel your top eyelid. It feels like a little fingernail clipping there at the edge. The cuts in Steps 13 and 14 highlight this structure.

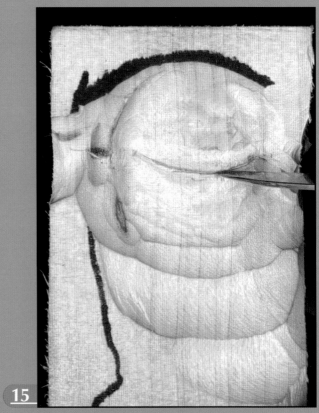

15

Using the carving knife, make a stop cut and relieve a small sliver of wood to create a shadow where the eyelids meet.

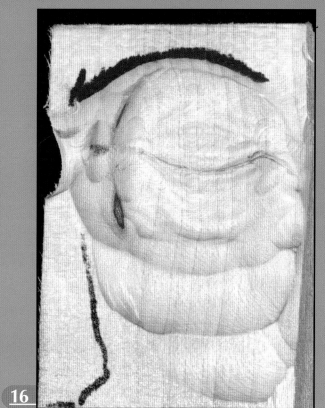

16 A close-up of the finished eye shows the slight separation between the eyelids and the structure of the cartilage in the lids themselves.

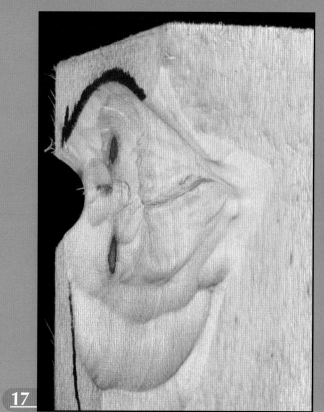

17 A view from the side clearly shows how the eye tilts into the face at an inward angle. Notice the simple, yet clear separation between the eyelids. This area is easy for a beginner to overdo. Only the smallest sliver of wood needs to be removed to make this eye look realistic.

Moving On: Practice, practice, practice. Carving eyes is a challenge; but with practice, you can become an expert. Work through all of the demonstrations in this book and follow the "Moving On" tips that I've provided at the end of each. Then take some classes or get together with other carvers at a carving club to hone your skills.

Diagram 1
Layout

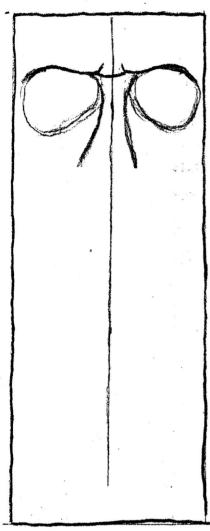

1. Mark the center line of the block.

2. Mark the brow bone and socket shape.

3. Mark the sides of the nose.

Side view after creating sockets.

Diagram 2
Socket Shape

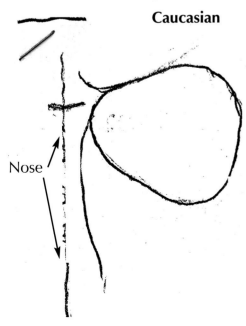

Caucasian

Nose

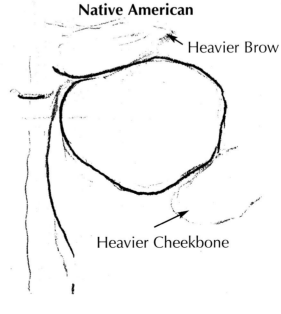

Native American

Heavier Brow

Heavier Cheekbone

Noted here are the differences between the two types of eye socket shapes for Caucasians and Native Americans. The change in eye shape is mostly due to the heavy cheekbone that is prominent in Native American faces.

Diagram 2 (cont)

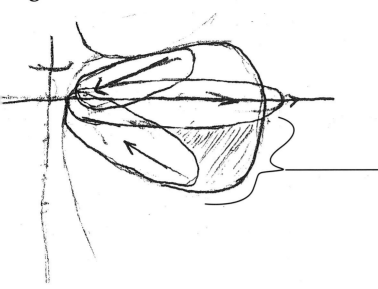

Soften and blend this area
out as shown in the
demonstration photographs.
The arrows show the
direction of the tool cut.

Diagram 3

Bridge and Nose

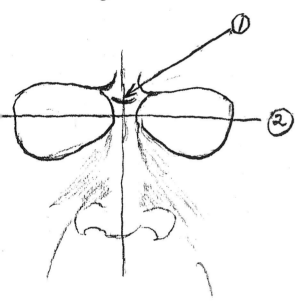

1. Dent in the bridge of the nose at the brow ridge.

2. The center of the eyes themselves. Note that the center of the eyes falls just slightly below the dent in the bridge of the nose.

Exercise: Look in the mirror. Take a pencil and place it horizontally on your face in the dent in the bridge of your nose. Observe how you can see just below the pencil without moving your eyes.

Diagram 4

Cross Section

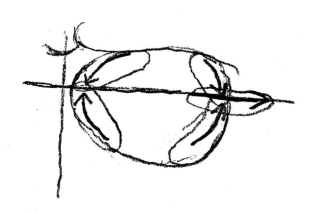

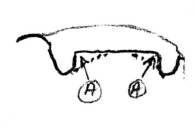

Note the sharp corners where the mound will be (A). These will be rounded and softened as the dotted line indicates. No wood is removed from the center.

Diagram 5
Surface Angle

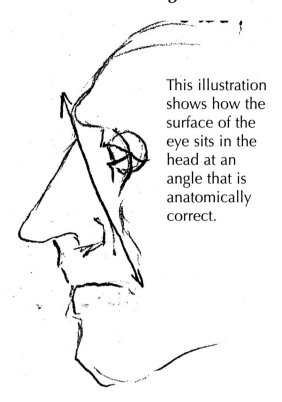

This illustration shows how the surface of the eye sits in the head at an angle that is anatomically correct.

Diagram 6
Eye Width

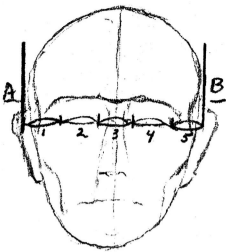

To figure the width of the eyes on your sculpture, measure from A to B, which is the widest part of the skull. This imaginary line is located just above the ears, not between the hollow of the temples.

Caucasians: 4.5 eyes wide
Native Americans: 5 eyes wide

As a carver, I am always aware of these guidelines and rules, but I myself do not actually measure the head before I do the eyes. If you have set up the area correctly and have followed the process outlined in this book, the eyes will fall within acceptable guidelines.

Diagram 7 - A
Eye Shape

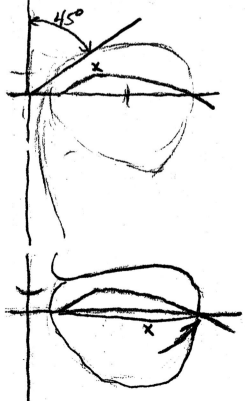

Top Eyelid
Notice where the lid rises from the inside corner at approximately 45° from the center of the face. The eyelid peaks at point X (before the middle of the eye), then drops gradually through the center line at the outside corner.

Bottom Eyelid
Notice that the bottom lid is basically the opposite of the top. It drops gradually, bottoms out at point X, the rises up to the top eyelid. The bottom eyelid tucks under the top eyelid at the outside corner (marked by an arrow).
Note that the distance from the center line of the eye to the top eyelid is quite a bit greater than the distance from the center line to the bottom eyelid. Reason: All movement of the eyelids takes place with the top lid; the bottom lid does not move. When blinking, the top eyelid comes down to meet the bottom.

Diagram 7 - B
Center Lines

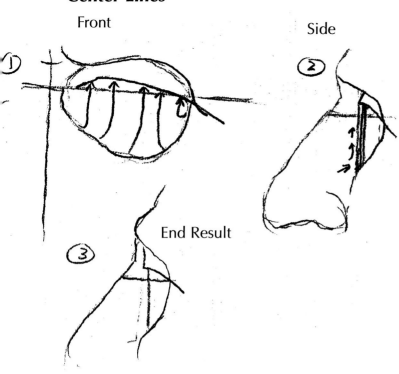

Front

Side

End Result

Make a stop-cut on the lid line. Cut in and straight up to the top lid, just enough to relieve the top lid. Maintain the roundness that was already established. Keep the thickness of the eyelid uniform from side to side on the top and the bottom lid.

Note: When drawing the center line of the eye, always extend the center line past the corners of the eye opening. Why? Because when you start cutting the eye openings, naturally the center line will be carved off, leaving no point of reference. A common mistake that happens when a carver redraws the center line after carving the top lid is to lower the center line, creating an eye that is too wide open. By extending the center line past the opening, two reference points will be left after the lid is carved. Just connect the two ends of the center line to make redrawing the original center line foolproof.

Diagram 7 - C
Cutting the Bottom Eyelid

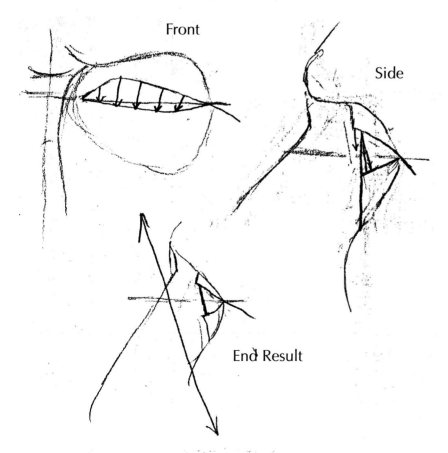

Front

Side

End Result

Make a stop cut on the bottom eyelid from corner to corner. From here on out, never cut up to the top lid again; all cuts are made from the top lid down to the bottom lid. Maintain the roundness from side to side and keep the lid at a uniform thickness.

Diagram 8
Pupils

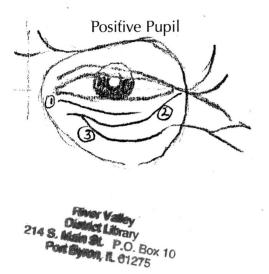

Positive Pupil

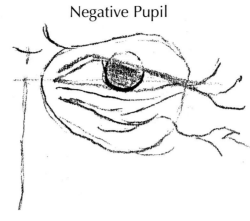

Negative Pupil

The two types of pupil treatments I like to use are positive and negative.

Positive Pupil: The pupil itself is intact and the iris or colored part of the eye is removed.

Negative Pupil: The pupil and iris area are all removed

Note: Never carve a pupil dead center in the middle of an eye. Always offset them to one side or the other, even the pupil is just slightly off center.

Diagram 9
Expression

A)

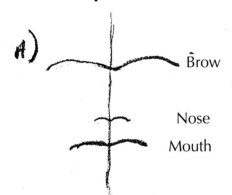

Brow

Nose

Mouth

B)

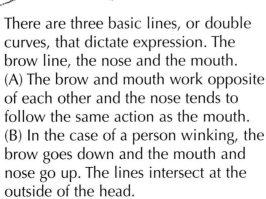

There are three basic lines, or double curves, that dictate expression. The brow line, the nose and the mouth.
(A) The brow and mouth work opposite of each other and the nose tends to follow the same action as the mouth.
(B) In the case of a person winking, the brow goes down and the mouth and nose go up. The lines intersect at the outside of the head.

Diagram 10
Sleeping or Closed Eye

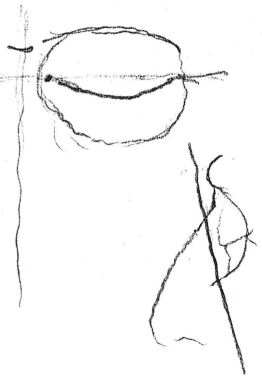

All of the muscles around the eye relax and the top lid drops to meet the bottom lid. Notice that the angle the eye in the head still remains the same as that of an open eye.